Sher Gill
The Living Master of '*The Way to God*'

THE WAY OF GOD

I AM THE WAY AND THE WAY IS WITHIN

SHER GILL

authorHOUSE®

AuthorHouse™ UK
1663 Liberty Drive
Bloomington, IN 47403 USA
www.authorhouse.co.uk
Phone: 0800.197.4150

Published by AuthorHouse 04/26/2019

ISBN: 978-1-7283-8754-3 (sc)
ISBN: 978-1-7283-8755-0 (hc)
ISBN: 978-1-7283-8753-6 (e)

First published by AuthorHouse: 10/12/2014

Print information available on the last page.

www.shergill.uk.com
Email: beingasaint@gmail.com

This book is dedicated
to all
Spiritual Seekers

CONTENTS

INTRODUCTION

The Way of God is especially written for the Seekers who want to feel the presence of God here and now. The message of God has been conveyed in very simple words. As you read along, the flow of Spirit will open up. If you are a disciple and follow the spiritual discipline, then there is nothing you cannot know or understand. All religions point to the fact that God is within, but we all fail to feel its presence because we fail to follow the way of God.

The first chapter of this book explains how to follow the way of God. *The Way of God* is an eye-opener for the true Seekers. It provides all the answers to common spiritual questions and helps Seekers find the truth. The way to God is very simple. It is only us who make it complicated. God is "The Soul", and so are you. So where is this barrier when you say, "I cannot do it"? I don't think I can use any simpler words than these: ***Just do it.*** We all are children of God, who loves us very dearly and is waiting for us with open arms.

I have experienced the presence of God this way and so can you. Each chapter is unique in its own way, and there is a clear message to let you feel how close you are to God. As you read, you will feel as if God is talking to you. Once you know the way of God, you will be the centre of all universes. There is a tremendous amount of God knowledge infused within each chapter. There is the history of known world prophets and religious track records. One chapter explores aliens, conveying information on their good looks and how their knowledge is beyond our physical judgement.

The physical universe is explained in depth, including knowledge of all of earth's fellow planets and how they affect our astrology charts. *The Way of God* explores how, due to these planetary and karmic effects, we experience the "wrath of God". You will be surprised to learn, asking yourself, where does this knowledge come from? It all comes from within our golden silence. After reading this book, you may find the key to opening this treasure and be part of great silence.

THE WAY OF GOD

This subject is very close to my heart. I don't think many people understand what it really means. We go around the subject and only want to know what it means from the surface level. Many people are aware that, if we apply the whole philosophy of God, it will not benefit us on a material basis. Many years ago, I advised someone to go for the whole instead of the parts. This person knew me very well and replied, "I know that you are going to be the future Master, so it is okay for you to be this serious.

But at present, it does not suit me." I said, "Fair enough, if that's what you believe." Mind you, this person is still struggling today. The clear message is that I am God, and so are you. Now the question is, "Are you? Unless and until you understand this concept, you will never have any serious spiritual success. You must know "My Way"—how and why I created this world and all the universes. To simply say that this is schooling for the soul is an under-statement.

You are part of this schooling. You are the student, and you are the teacher. You are part of the universe, and you are the universe. You are learning within this universe, and at the same time, you are running this universe. I am the experience, and I experience myself through each of you. The whole of creation was made for a purpose. There is not a single atom that is worthless. I have given free will to each of you to live your lives on your terms and suffer accordingly.

There are many species that are known to be dangerous to humans—some snakes, for example. Even hearing the word *snake* or seeing one in the garden causes many people to shiver. In the past, you were one of them too. You may never know how many people you have bitten and who has died from your poison. Rats are known to spread disease, and mosquitoes can spread malaria. The bees sting, but at the same time, they provide us with honey.

Nowadays, we make artificial honey, but it is never the same in taste and far from the natural properties of the real thing. Salt and chilli are for other experiences. This is to give you the taste of everything and enable you to experience all there is from every possible angle you can think of as a soul. The day you understand my way is the day that all your questions will cease. Your questions and complaints are the result of not understanding me - God. We pray to God or Master or Spirit for others to change mentally to please us.

This is not going to happen. Praying for this means you do not understand my way. You never know, the other person may be acting under my instructions to polish your state of consciousness. Or the interaction between the two of you could be a very important experience for that soul too, and it cannot be altered to please you. This world, atmosphere, people, and animals are not going to change to satisfy you. You better change yourself and learn to adjust accordingly or suffer.

I am God. Are you?

The only difference between you and me is how you understand this sentence. Very recently, a person came to see me and said he was requesting Spirit to make one of his relatives behave "gently" towards him. No change of this kind is going to happen. You see, this is where we all go wrong. You never know how difficult a time you may have given this soul in the past. Or it could be a new account to be settled in the future. I am not very proud of my family, apart from my grand-parents.

All others were stationed at a perfect place to strike with their spikes at every opportunity. Hell was created around me to test me from every angle you could think of. I lived within this hell, and still I continued to recite the word of God all the time. I did not let them affect my spiritual goal because I did not let these monkeys make a circle around me, as I will mention in another chapter. The word *monkey* is a symbol of the negative power in action.

I will not use this word for any humans, as others I have interacted with were experiencing life from a different angle than I was. They may not be aware for what purpose they were used. This is exactly what I said in my discourses of disciple and discipline. These discourses came from my personal experiences. One of the virtues of God is that God does not react. Therefore, do not expect God to punish someone because he or she has done something wrong to you.

Leave the execution to the person appointed by God---that is, Dharam-Raj, or the King of the Dead—for any action. The punishment will take place when all the learning conditions are perfect for that soul. There is no such experience that I have not been through. You must learn to let it be. This applies to you and all others. You must take every situation as the will of God. Silence is golden. It can help us to go through hard experiences with ease.

Sometimes we make situations worse than they are or are supposed to be with our lack of command over physical actions or spoken words. For some, it may be a good idea to have a silence fast once a week. It can help to calm down your mental activity, and while you are silent, Spirit may begin to flow more freely. I am going to give you a spiritual exercise to practise. It has never been given before. Do not take this exercise as an ego boost. If you do, it means you did not understand my message in this discourse.

Just for a day, think of yourself as being in the position of God.

If you were God, considering every situation during the day—good or bad—what would you do? How would you react? You will be surprised to learn the answers to these questions. God does not react to any situation. It does not matter how bad things may be. God does not suffer either. Take it as an experience. In the physical sense, if someone hurts you, God gets hurt because you are part of God. But if you hurt someone else, then it also hurts God because the other person is also part of God.

Now, having this knowledge, I am sure you will not hurt anyone. God experiences every situation through each of us. Every action hits God directly. We are being used as foliage on the surface but continue to complain. You are an individual who can explore the universe as a soul. Yet you are also part of it within God's experience. Now you know to what extent we under-estimate ourselves and walk into the traps of Kal.

This is exactly what happens when a young person walks into the trap of a relationship or a friendship that uses the lure of sweet talk or back-stabbing and leaves his or her family as a result. Sometimes it may take many years to learn that it was a trap. On realisation and returning, the family accepts the person again with open arms. In the same way, God is always waiting for you, no questions asked, because he knows that it is all part of the learning process.

You might conclude that God is neutral and does not respond to any situation. God is beyond the emotional state, and you have acquired the same qualities as well. Can you imagine the state of consciousness you have just accomplished? The word *unfoldment* has been used by Paul Ji quite often to express that there is no thing or situation a soul does not have the knowledge of as part of God. But during its journey into the lower worlds, a soul must unfold to every available situation for training.

In order to attain the full knowledge—that is to experience the totality created by God for us and become the knowers and part of the scheme of God as assistants. Many different mottos have been used, such as "A Way of life". These mottos change every decade, but we cannot twist the teachings to satisfy people's minds. We have seen the results over the last forty years; they have not been very fruitful. The "Wind" can blow only for a certain period of time, as it has its limits too.

God is omnipotent, omniscient, and omnipresent. God is, has been, and will always be the same—total and the whole of totality. It is we who have been sent into the lower worlds for schooling. The training ground has been prepared for your experience or enlightenment. So do not expect changes to suit your preferences. I would rather give you a hard and distasteful medicine to swallow. All this goody-goody talks or writing has been our failure. I do not wish to see anyone fail who believes in me.

It is not you who has failed. I will take it as my failure if I am unable to convey the message of God in the proper way. There is no other teaching I am aware of that gives the message of God in this manner. Many of the world's spiritual leaders would not have a clue what I am talking about here. They lead the masses to prayer, which means their followers directly or indirectly beg for something. When they should instead be guiding their congregations to work off or balance their karmic load in order to have better lives.

The majority of these leaders are interested only in financial gain in their accounts at the expense of their followers. That is their reward for the hard work they do for their followers. I do not ask for money from anyone nor do I accept any donations. But some people feel that it is their religious obligation to give donations. My reward from you will be, your spiritual success, as you have become 'the master of your universe'. Please put yourself in the shoes of God.

You will come to know how flexible you have become. You will let go of whatever it may be. Be yourself and do not interfere in any situation created by it (God). You are flexible, you are forgiving, you are silent, and you are totally neutral, as is God. You will experience the total calm within yourself. Total happiness is an understatement. You will be sitting within the spiritual pool created by God, and your knowingness will be beyond description.

This will be the first time you will experience a saying you have heard many times over the last forty years. "You live in this world but are not a part of it." Before it was just a saying, but now you will be in this experience. You have to create this situation to experience the scheme of God. Guess what? You cannot even guess what you are going to experience.

Try to maintain this state of consciousness on a daily basis. I will not be surprised to hear from you one day, "I am the Master." My spiritual goal is accomplished. This is exactly what God wants from each of us—to become the knowers of truth and feel ourselves as part of it. Now consciously say:

I am it, and it is me, and we are one.
Now I know the one,
To whom, no one knows, but now it knows **me**.

The majority of you are trying to know me by reciting the verses of the Qur'an, the Bible, or the text of Hinduism or any other "isms". These passages are all talking about religion but not about God. By reciting and trying to understand the verses, you can or will become like the priests or scholars who wrote them, but you'll never become like me. These writings are only for guidance. I live within those who are pure in their hearts and are down-to-earth people, as I am.

I live within those who approach me directly through the Master. Your problems will never be solved and your cries will never be heard until you begin to listen to me and are conquered by Spirit. At the moment, you are very similar to a wild horse. That will not let anyone sit on its back until it is broken by the horse trainer. You may struggle if you wish. I have given you "free will". But until you say to Spirit, "Please do whatever you wish to do with me; I am at your service," you will struggle.

At this moment, you are not practising the concept of "letting it go". Or maybe you are letting it go but, at the same time, you want to hold onto everything. These two points do not go together. You are a raw material like clay, which needs to be moulded to take any shape. A toy can be made, or it can be shaped into a brick. Let me mould you. Whether the shape you take be toy or a brick, be flexible, as I am.

And all will be yours, and you will open the gates of heaven to others—to let them know, who I am and where I am. I am so close to you all, as I am God. God has given this message for you all through me, as I am the open channel for Spirit, and so are you. Make the most of your time. It is never too late. After reading this discourse, you can moan and groan or act happy-go-lucky. The ball is in your court.

Spirit loves you, as you are part of it.

DWELLING WITHIN

We are always seeking God in temples or churches—when it is sitting right within us. And no one wants to know this truth because we have no insight into it, and we are not taught this way. Someone can only tell us if they have personal experience. When we are in trouble or in some kind of desperate need, we go anywhere to pray. We have come to a point in Kali-Yuga where we feel God is millions of miles away and out of reach.

Over the millennia, we have lost this connection and awareness of the inner presence of God, and our approach to life has become more or less materialistic. Over the years, I have come across many people who have asked, "What God? Where is God? Has anyone seen God? Can you show me where God is?" These people are not wrong to raise these types of questions. Their reasons for questioning the presence of God are many— the environment they are living in or the way life has treated them, for example.

There are situations when a saint or a good person suffers at the hands of villains, but the villains are having a good time and living a prosperous life. After witnessing such circumstances, many people will lose their faith and ask similar questions about the nature and existence of God. These situations do occur. And in some circumstances, they may be a lesson in disguise for the villains. Such lesson may not materialise instantly, but it will shine through in later years.

Many times, saints do set up these examples to show people how to obey the will of God and let it be, when they could have done anything to teach a lesson to the people involved. Saints leave "punishment" in the hands of Spirit on a neutral basis. When it comes to punishment given by Spirit, whether it be instantly or in later years, the saints do not get involved. They are beyond being "for or against" any situation. They are examples of patience and tolerance.

Jesus Christ could have escaped if he wanted to, but he did not. This is why we know him today. Otherwise, we, in terms of history, wouldn't know who he was. Sikhism is full of examples. The fifth Guru, Arjan Dev, sat on a hot metal-plate, over a heated clay oven, while the Muslim captors poured heated sand over his head. Despite the pain, he continued to recite holy chants throughout this ordeal. So, what gave him the strength to suffer without uttering a single word against the people who tortured him?

This is an example of a saint who was connected to the divine light and sound and had a direct link with God. Now, whether you see God at work or not depends on your state of consciousness. It was Arjan Dev's inner strength or connection with Spirit at work. Unless we have this inner connection, we will never be called saints. With book knowledge, we are known as priests or scholars. To be in connection with or to be known by Spirit is most important.

We should try in this lifetime, or the opportunity may arise in future lives when we have earned good karma. On the basis of our good karma, we express our individuality, and that will be our state of consciousness. We come to a point in life where our spiritual mind seeks some "outer" teacher or teachings. These newfound teachings may lead the individual to have an esoteric experience. This urge within leads you from one teacher to another until you are satisfied or your destiny leads you to the teachings appointed by the lord of karma.

Also, at times, Spirit leads you under the instructions of God itself, so you can lead the people of some religion in the future. Any Master or teachings that do not lead you to the inner teachings are not worth following. Your spiritual journey will be at a standstill; another lifetime will be wasted, as if living like a vegetable. The outer teachings give insight into what to ponder upon when you are imagining the "inner".

Whatever you have read over the years is good. But now it is your own efforts and responsibility of the Master to lead you to the inner. Here are the answers for whatever you have been seeking in life. Now is the time to reap whatever you have sown over the years spiritually. To become the knower of inner worlds, you have to build a relationship with your spiritual Master first. Otherwise your journey or dream will be at a standstill. The basic steps are:

1. Do your meditation regularly with full sincerity.
2. Have total reliance upon the spiritual Master.
3. Practise presence and communicate with the spiritual Master in your own way.

Inner communication

The Master should be able to operate physically and at the inner level. Physically, he is limited, as he cannot be with everyone at the same time. But spiritually he can be anywhere and with everyone as required depending on the situation. Despite your meditation, you should try to maintain inner communication with the spiritual Master all the time. As I mention often, I only met my guru physically a maximum of ten times over the span of thirty years.

But I never lost sight of him even once spiritually, as I learned that it is very important to build this inner relationship. The majority of members failed on this point and tried to be known by the Master on a physical level. Perhaps that is all they achieved, and they lost that as well in later years. With this inner communication, it becomes very easy for the Master to teach the Seeker; there is no use of verbal words, and the mind is also set aside.

Then the silent language becomes very powerful and pure in nature. It is beyond the reach of any physical means, and the teachings are given directly to soul. It will be a natural process for the recipient, but it could become a

Sher Gill

phenomenon to the normal human mind. It is this inner communication that will lead you to become the master of your own universe. Once this communication is established, you will operate from the level of sun and moon worlds in astral plane.

This state of consciousness is required to contact the spiritual Master during the spiritual exercises, so the Master can lead you to the inner or higher planes. The person with this ability can roam freely in the upper regions. As a regular visitor, even without the Master, you have built your own authority, as you are recognised by the lords of these planes. Now you can communicate with spiritual Master, as well as with all the lords of higher planes.

Now you have become the authority and can take others with you on an inner journey. You can help someone who is stuck in these planes; at the mention of your name, he or she will be set free. This communication will lead you into the presence of Satnam Ji. Once you have become Self-Realised, you understand that it is a practical experience, and you will have met all the conditions of roaming freely at your own volition. Now it is time to explore the worlds of being.

You have the blessings of Satnam Ji. During the daytime, it is your own effort that will maintain this state of consciousness. At night-time, it becomes very easy for the Master to take you on dream travels, as you are an open channel for Spirit all the time. Once this process is continuous over twenty-four hours, can you imagine your progress? This can lead you to God-Realisation and into the presence of God. You will have proven this "Reality" to yourself.

Without this inner channel, nothing is possible. It is due to this communication that all the secret teachings are made available. These secret teachings prepare the Seeker for the highway to the higher worlds. Now you will notice that your material and emotional life begins to slip to the side, and your soul shines out and is reflected in your aura. Others will notice and wonder what it could be. It is through this inner vision that all the inner worlds, which are beyond the physical, come into focus.

The inner worlds are as real as the physical world is real to our physical senses. The surrender to the Master also happens on the inner level, and the outer level just follows. When everything is alive at the inner level, then, who is interested in the outer level? The presence of the Master or Spirit is felt when the inner level is active. Nothing is possible unless we leave our physical shell. This inner strength is responsible for overpowering negative habits, such as alcohol or hard drugs, or controlling depression.

The inner is also responsible for the origin of mystic powers. To the saints, such powers are normal. But to others, they are miracles. Once you are successful at the inner level, it is also known as soul travel. Many other achievements are natural, among them healings and telepathy. With this inner connection, reality shines and illusion dis-appears.

ARE YOU A GARDENER?

This is a self-analysis for any spiritual Seeker. Are we doing enough homework concerning our state of consciousness? We have a responsibility to maintain it to the highest ethics—to be an example to the others. We are the representatives of true and pure teachings in this world. Many years ago, when we joined this path as Seekers of spiritual freedom, we were taught some basic principles to follow. This included keeping our thoughts pure and simple.

It also meant working towards balancing the five passions of our mind. These passions are the cause for our excessive desires and future sufferings. A gardener who looks after his or her garden makes sure the texture of the soil and the seeds, he or she wants to plant are suitable. Once the seeds are planted, they are watered at regular intervals, and the first petals appear. It does not take long, for a seedling to grow into many branches.

To have good crops, the gardener is very watchful for any weeds growing alongside the plant. If weeds do grow, the gardener will either pull them out by hand or use some chemicals to eliminate them. The weeds growing alongside the plant will use part of the strength of the soil that is supporting the plants. The plants growing alongside the weeds will not be as healthy or fruitful as expected. If we need to travel into the other or inner worlds, we have to drop lots of physical garbage or baggage.

Such baggage is constantly pulling us down, similar to the effect of gravity on planet Earth. This is a training ground for soul, so everything has been designed to provide the pull—to keep us anchored to this world or in the shackles of the negative power. After all these years of following, we have become too relaxed and forgotten our true goal, which was to free ourselves forever from the wheel of eighty-four. There is one basic principle in order to accomplish this freedom—to learn to set free the others.

We must set free those who are around us as part of our family or as friends. When we are sincere about the teachings, we try to follow all of the dos or don'ts to achieve success. To work on our weaknesses is a responsibility for life; otherwise, we are wasting our teacher's valuable time. Many people do not realise that this teaching has been designed to train the individual into sainthood. It is not a religion, which is controlled by many systems or politics up to some extent.

A few Seekers are totally trapped by the Kal and act their part in our teachings on political grounds. Since I have been given the spiritual responsibility to teach whoever comes my way as a true Seeker, I will do my best on the inner realm, which is beyond limits. I will give physical assistance as much as I possibly can, as there are so many limits on the physical world. Masters are not born every day. Their birth takes place under the supervision of Satnam Ji and God.

The birth may not be as dramatic as mentioned by many religions. Tales of a Master being born out of wedlock to a virgin mother or appearing alongside the mother's bed are all mythological stories. But definitely Masters are born at the right time and in the family where the teachings can be given when required. This child will have a guardian angel from birth. There will be three or four saints of different age groups in this world at all times to fulfil this responsibility.

The living Master does not have to die physically to pass over the responsibility. He can retire at a certain age when the next person is ready to take the responsibility. The third person can be in his teens or early twenties, preparing to take the approaching responsibility. It is possible that the fourth in line has just been born or is on the way to this earth planet to take the responsibility at the command of Spirit. No one has control over these individuals apart from God itself.

There is not even any present Master who has any control over the giving, or not, of this responsibility. As this individual is born especially for this purpose, the present Master has to hand over the responsibility according to the time allotted by Spirit. In turn, the next one will step in when the time arrives. This procedure is perfectly and whole-heartedly executed with the full blessings and support of the departing Master.

Any assistance required in the future will be given, as these Masters are here to fulfil the command of God, not to create mental barriers. The master-ship will not remain in one country forever or within one race of people. It will change from one continent to the next as required by God. The master-ship remaining in one place does not benefit the whole world. If it remains in one country, the people will begin to claim it as theirs to keep. This way, pure teachings automatically turn into religion.

It is better, for the good of the whole, for the present Master to pass the spiritual mantle in time to the new recipient. Due to unforeseen circumstances, Spirit will give it to the new Master in whatever country, he is residing. These teachings are designed for universal purpose, as God is dwelling everywhere. Now, I will bring the state of consciousness into the limelight, held by our long-term members. I know some of them who are in the teachings since the time of Paul Ji.

And definitely from the early days of Darwin. When I joined the teachings in 1976, if I recall, some of them were members of "The Way to God" at that time. Spending all these years on this path, they could have been as good as any saint. Ever since I released my book *The Way to God*, some of them—I do not wish to name them, but I know who they are—have been sending me dirty, degrading, and abusive emails. I am under the direction of Spirit, and I am not purposely creating any threat to any person in this world.

After reading my book, these individuals must be experiencing some threat within and are on the attack through the medium of the internet. Now the question arises, after all these years, what have they learned? As far as I am concerned, they have learned "nothing". I want to make one point very clear about the spiritual initiations. Any person who does any overt negative act against any individual will lose his or her initiations right on the spot.

It does not matter which Master has initiated you. The initiation is just an indication that an individual can maintain his or her state of consciousness at the level of that initiation and can keep striving for the next step. Since negative thoughts originated in your mind, you automatically dropped from your state of consciousness. If this state of consciousness is not maintained, you drop like a brick to the ground. On this path, you must be watchful before taking any step.

The Kal is working from all corners and is ready to trap you. To make any progress, we must be alert all the time so as not to fail. To maintain this state of consciousness is our responsibility. Keep asking yourself this question: *Am I a good gardener?* God has infinite qualities—that is, totality. Through your spiritual endeavours, the number of its qualities you have adopted or can maintain throughout will be your state of consciousness.

This is how we differ from each other; otherwise, as souls we are all the same. The more qualities we adopt, the closer we are to God. One day you will realise you are receiving direct answers before even asking a question.

You are never alone; the Spirit is with you always,

SATSANG

For Satsang, there are some guidelines to be followed so as to have successful spiritual gathering:

We must arrive at our Satsang place on time. As a rule, we close the door five minutes before commencing the Satsang.

Once all members have arrived, during the first five minutes, the "teacher" will leave the room for two to three minutes. 'Teacher' while you are physically alone, you will chant your own spiritual word silently. That is called tuning with Spirit. When you feel the inner nudge indicating that you are ready, walk inside the room. You will feel that the Spirit or the inner Master has taken over. The experience for the "teacher" and all the participants will be beyond physical.

We begin with 'Haiome' a spiritual chant, for one to two minutes. This will help us to relax physically and raise our vibrations spiritually.

The chapter we are going to read or discuss must have been read at home prior to Satsang. That way, during the Satsang, we can understand the message thoroughly.

Everyone must participate by reading a paragraph and explaining the message in that paragraph. If unsure, you can request that the teacher explain it further.

The time for the Satsang is one hour or no more than one and a half hours.

You must stay within the subject that is being discussed on the day.

After the agreed time by all the members, you may close the Satsang with the same spiritual chant.

"May the blessing be" or "Sarbat-da-Bhala" both hold the same meaning so you can use either.

After the conclusion of Satsang, you may have a cup of tea. During that time, you can discuss, share, or ask any question regarding the teachings. But no social gatherings or any other topics are to be discussed.

Contemplate on all the points we have learned. It will help to refine our spiritual self to unfold further or to become aware of what we already have.

DISCIPLE

Are you a disciple? Yes, indeed you are. But at the same time, you are the future Master too. This is the point that you need to keep your focus on. Every person is a born Master, as we have all the qualities of God within us. But we have turned ourselves into the ways of Kal. The reasons for doing so are many—the bad karma we have created, knowingly or unknowingly. In either case, we are responsible for our doings. Every waking moment has to be lived consciously.

Now I will give you an example. How you can do this? I am sure the majority of you have seen the movie *Silent Flute*. There was a Seeker who wanted to know the truth. The journey is from the physical plane to the soul plane. The Seeker was willing to go through any test to have the experience. It was partly written by Bruce Lee, so the whole journey is expressed through kung-fu or martial arts. At one point of the journey, he was attacked by a number of monkeys, representing the negative power.

The monkeys were trying to circle around him. He had been guided by his Master never to let the monkeys circle around him; once they do, the Master had said, they will attack you. The Seeker remembered his Master's guidance. As the monkeys tried to circle around him, he kept turning around with them. His Master had also told him to keep eye contact with them. Once they know that you were not looking at them, they would attack. The Seeker kept turning around and maintained eye contact with them all the time.

After a long time, the monkeys gave up. The Seeker succeeded in his efforts. And the Master prepared him for the next step. I am sure you got the message, but you have to make the effort to succeed in your spiritual journey. Many times, we create the situations we face ourselves, with a "don't-care attitude". And many are helping the negative forces to make a number of circles around them in a day. This is very easily done.

When you have plenty of time at hand and indulge yourself in self-created or natural physical problems, this is what you do. You go over and over your problem. The number of times you go over your problems is the number of circles the negative power has made around you. This is what we have to be watchful for. During the time you are going over your problems, you are a clear channel for the negative force. Pure Spirit cannot penetrate within your circle to help you because you are not letting it help.

Do not let the Kal force circle around you. We all have problems. Request Spirit to resolve the problem, and it will be done, provided you don't make another circle around it. Spirit will help. If not, let it be and move on with your life. Do not stand still. That is not very fruitful. This is why there are so many pending unsolved problems with so many followers; people do not let go of the situations they find themselves in. We have one chapter "Let It Go" in our book "The Way to God" dedicated to this concept.

I could have written a complete book on the subject if I had mentioned all the situations I have been through. Instead, I summed up the entire subject in three paragraphs. The less said the better. Do not help the Kal force make circles around you. This is the responsibility of the disciple. Early on, you set up a spiritual goal to achieve in this life. Now there is no looking back—no letting any situation interfere with your goal. I know you are not a failure, so do not let the Kal force fail you.

In effect, the Kal force is not here to fail you. I will take it as a blessing in disguise. The Kal force is helping you to build up your spiritual stamina. You want to graduate, but you do not want to pass any exams. If you do not pass any exams, how will you consider yourself qualified? I will give you another example on the same subject. You can choose one that suits you. In my village, many beggars come to beg for food or money, and in almost every house there is a dog left loose within the boundary walls for security purposes.

If the beggars got scared of dogs, then they would be empty-handed all day. One day, a beggar came to our house. For some unknown reason, I kept looking at him and watched him for almost two minutes. I learned something from him. As he entered the main gate, he made his call for alms. The dog became alert and came near the beggar to bark and attack. This was the learning point, because there was something keeping the dog at bay.

I noticed that the beggar had a long stick held under his armpit, pointing about two feet behind his legs. The beggar never stood still. He kept moving his upper body, a quarter of a turn to the left or right continuously. The dog kept barking and attacking but was strangely deceived by the movement of the stick. The dog was following the stick as it moved from left to right in a circle. The beggar got his alms (*bhiksha*) and went to the next house for the same purpose. The dog was deceived by this artful dodger.

You can find your own way of stopping the Kal force from making a circle around you. You are never short of ideas. God has given you all the creative faculties to use, which we hardly use. I know some Seekers who are not feeling well physically. Many times, I advise them that they can do this or that. You are the first person to know that there is something wrong with your physical body. The doctor will come to know only when you approach him or her.

Analyse the symptoms and work around them. There are many situations where you can use self-help remedies. I ask the same person, "Did you do something about it?" In return, all I get is a smile. I am sure that you know the answer. As a disciple, you have the responsibility to look after your body. The body is known as a physical temple because your soul is residing within. Physically, if you feel well, you can meditate better.

If you are in some kind of pain or uneasiness, it will reflect during your meditation sitting. To have the best results when meditating, you should feel on top of the world, carefree, and happy. Feel that you are the only person on this planet earth because you are going to be in the presence of Spirit—God. How can you meet God when there are so many obstacles in the way? I am sure now you know what kind of feelings or attitude you require when meeting God. Make your guru proud.

I am sure my guru was proud of me. He used to give me hard times on purpose, when there was no need, which I do not do. That's why I used to get upset. I used to challenge him to find any fault or weakness in me. Can you claim this? Yes, you can. If I can, so can you. There are some examples of saints in our discourse on *Bhakti marg*. These are the people who left behind all their relations and belongings to materialise their goal.

We do not have to practise this way of life, and we can create a balanced feeling within ourselves while being at home. Those saints were sitting or standing for lengthy hours to find the focus at the spiritual eye. There is nothing that is beyond your reach. Once you know, it will be like a toy to any child. You will not even notice when you are within the physical body or outside of it because you will have become part of Spirit. This will be your shining moment, when you say, "I am. I am. I am Spirit!"

DISCIPLINE

Discipline is the backbone of our success. Every person is very much aware of this, as it has been mentioned many times. Discipline covers most of the activities of the day. Spirit will help with what we need to achieve as our goal. The mental arena is responsible for our clever or misleading situations. That which is causal can drag you into certain unpleasant memories. The astral plane is our emotional factor, and it can create many unwanted obstacles that can be painful at a later date.

The physical body only acts by following the dictates of the above and experiences pain. The main obstacle we find here is our mind. But with efforts, we can train this mind to act as a spiritual mind. Then it will have or create spiritual thoughts. I have given many examples of how to do this training in the past. Some examples include regular meditation, mental fasting, doing good deeds, and being in the company of good or positive people.

Never let an iota of negative thinking come into your mind. This means, you have to be very alert all the time. Keep your focus on staying positive in your thoughts and actions. After a while, you will notice that you have completely lost your focus and are wandering many miles away. Do not worry. Once you come to this realisation, forget about the lost time. Worrying about it will not turn the clock back. Make a fresh start. I have been through all this.

It may seem a struggle in the beginning. But eventually, you will be the winner. Once your mind begins to originate spiritual thoughts, it will be out of your control because it will only have spiritual thoughts, even if you want to have other thoughts. I experimented with this long ago, once my mind was trained and I was living a very positive life, spiritually as well as physically. Many times, I was so carried away with spirit it took me a few hours to realise physically where I was.

Then I would think, *I'd better make another fresh start.* After a little analysis, I would realise that I had been in the spiritual fountain all the time. So what fresh start was I talking about? All my physical chores were looked after by Spirit and executed to perfection. I was working on a printing machine, where all the printing details were very important, and I was known as the best printer. I used to feed cardboards into the machine—a two-person job, at least.

However, I was doing it alone very successfully. At the same time, I was writing down spiritual notes that Spirit was dictating to me. These notes are still sitting in my files. I was revising our spiritual discourses as well. You may be wondering how many jobs I was doing in one go. I don't know myself. This is the beauty of Spirit. Once you are tuned into Spirit, you cross all the limits. And then, even if you try, you cannot control your spiritual thoughts. Now they control you.

Very similarly, if negative thoughts are controlling you at present, you may be saying, "Sher Gill is giving us many examples, but I cannot do it." There is nothing in this world or beyond that you cannot do. Nothing is impossible. I removed this word from my life when I was very young—at least on the day I came in contact with Darwin physically and our spiritual journey and friendship began. Once you are tuned into Spirit, your life will operate from a different angle.

You have never dreamed of this before. You will say, "How did I manage to miss all this?" Now you are trying to take responsibility for your life, physically and mentally. That is why it is beyond your control. Everything you do is limited within the lower worlds. Once Spirit takes over, all your responsibilities are under the command of Spirit. All your chores are done with minimum effort, and your problems start to vanish into thin air.

Those problems that still linger in some corners of your life do not bother you as much, because now you have become more powerful than them. You have to train your mind to stay positive all the time. I received a very positive e-mail from Mr Raj Paul of Canada. He mentioned that he was trying his best to keep his thoughts positive and was putting effort into reading this book in his spare time. You can learn something from this young man.

He is trying to keep his mind occupied with spiritual thoughts. This is how you train your mind. To discipline yourself is the key. There are no hard and fast rules about what you should do. This is the beauty of this spiritual path. There are some dos and don'ts, as long as they are positive and spiritual. Those who have no dos and don'ts in life run wild and do worse. This is the point many people have overlooked in the past. Create your own strategies for disciplining your thoughts and physical actions at the same time.

I created my own ways of doing this, and I have crossed all the limits. The majority of our present religious scriptures mention that there are a few experiences they say no human being can have. With my efforts and sincerity towards Spirit, I have proved them wrong. One day, I will put these experiences in writing. Many people have not even scratched the surface of the first step. I am always around to help spiritually, as well as physically to guide at a surface level. This opportunity should not be missed at any cost.

However, I do not want anyone to do such acts that may put him or her out of balance. In 'The Way to God', I mentioned in the very last line of the chapter called "God-Realisation" that, in my terminology, you have to walk even over yourself! Many people don't even want to lose a small coin, yet they expect the sky to fall for them. You have to be daring and adventuresome. You do whatever is possible in your power and leave the rest in the hands of Spirit to take over. God will not fail you.

CHILDREN OF GOD

Sometimes I wonder, are we are good-for-nothings as the English saying goes? After all, we all believe that God is our father and we are the sons or daughters of God respectively. Yet we are nowhere near having the qualities held by our father or parent God. No one can even think in these terms or pause for a minute to analyse the real question: What we are doing and asking, is it really worth it? We have no direction in life whatsoever. What we are doing?

We are more or less puzzled and leading our lives as if others are leading or as we have been told to do by our elders. We have created the lower worlds as a battleground, instead of staying in balance and enjoying the nature of having our beings here and progressing spiritually. We have such a responsibility on our shoulders to maintain the well-being of all the universes. First, we have to maintain our vibrations spiritually in a balanced state.

Secondly, we have to create our ability as the children of God to come and go in the presence of God. It is our right as the children of God, and God has invested the ability within us. It is expecting us to unfold ourselves to this ability and become assistants as teachers in the lower worlds. This means helping others in what you know and acting as assistants in the higher worlds to assist the newcomers and show them around.

This is so that they can learn further and become the knowers of truth and let others know that it is possible. Once you are a frequent visitor to the higher planes and you have seen the ecstasy experiences or the glittering visions of the higher worlds, you will never hesitate to leave this world. I think that the people around you should be lucky that you are living among them. We have to follow the golden rule that is to keep your silence.

I know that most of the time people don't even notice who you are and what your business is. People are too busy earning their living to make ends meet on a daily basis. We might hear the odd remark, "Oh, yes. He is a good and honest man." But rarely do we hear anything further than that. You cannot even express yourself freely to let others know who you are. The remarks will be along the lines of, "He is mentally disturbed or depressed," or, "He is following some cult teachings."

They will decide to leave you alone, as you are not following the traditional religion. Sometimes I wonder, what religion are they following? I will be glad to know if someone is following any religion seriously. If we do, we will have saints everywhere. All the religious scriptures convey the same message. All the religious books are written in such a manner that, if you read or follow them seriously, you are bound to become a saint in your own right.

We are led to believe by our elders or religious leaders that we must read a page or two on a daily basis. Some are repeating this process five times a day. This should bring the discipline on a physical level, but do we gain anything on a spiritual level? Most likely, the answer is no. One *word* is good enough if meditated on properly on a daily basis. In my early life, I learned the first twenty-four words of the Guru-Granth of Sikhism or known as the first portion of 'Japji-Sahib'.

I believe that, if you contemplate on these few words, they are more than good enough to lead you into the presence of God. On the basis of those twenty-four words, I have managed to write five spiritual books, or nearly one thousand pages. Many times, I give this example to those who are willing to listen, which is a physical expression. The spiritual way is also the same, but we try to ignore it by saying that it is not possible; we have been trained in the art of dying (death) instead of living.

I wonder sometimes, why have we, gone away from reality? Why have we indulged in every activity of illusion? All these worlds are "Intact" because everything is created in balance. So how come we see the followers of illusion everywhere? There is a saying in English: "If you can't beat them, join them." By not joining the masses, the odd person will suffer at the hands of others—unless he or she is strong enough to face the whole world, if needs be. Being alone but spiritually awakened, we are strong.

Coming back to the physical example earlier, we as parents try to educate our children as much possible, so they can make their way in this world smoothly and successfully. One valuable point to be noted here is that, we all try and make sure that our children are more educated and successful than we are. The same procedure is followed generation after generation and all through this world. It makes me wonder, as we are the children of God, what God may be thinking about us.

This is a physical expression as God is always in the beingness state. God sends forth its representatives or prophets all the time to teach us and to make us aware of our true identity and our spiritual ability. Living in the illusionary world, we are so busy solving our domestic problems, we turn a blind eye to our spiritual abilities and ignore them completely, saying they are beyond our reach. If someone is spiritually successful, we call the person a "saint".

With our problems, we go and sit by this saint's feet. It is our belief that he will sort out our problems. He is no better a person than you are, his soul is not superior to yours, apart from his awareness of reality. And this awareness he has gained or unfolded through his spiritual endeavour. I have come to the conclusion that every person in the whole world has given up hope of being in the presence of God. Today in the scientific world, if there was any hope, that is also fading away.

"God" our father also wants to educate us as much as possible, so we can assist in God worlds—just as we do in this world, helping our parents when needed. We always under-estimate our abilities, when we can progress spiritually so much more than we can ever imagine because we have similar qualities as our creator, God. Once you accomplished your spiritual goal, you will say to yourself, "I am it, and it is me!" That will be the total awareness of soul.

There is only one God. Neither I nor you can ever be a second God. But with this awareness, you will feel close to it, as you are part of it. Of-course you are! This is the only reason to send all the souls into the lower worlds—to educate ourselves to become aware of our true identity, "children of God". So, from now on, you had better start to act as one in order to be counted in the scheme of God. Now you are not the assistant of God but the son or daughter of God. As soul, you are part of it.

GOD IS CALLING YOU

God has many ways of communicating with its creation; so, does its creation have many ways of communicating. It is silent communication; at the same time, it is verbal too. You may be wondering, what could it be? It is divine light and sound. There are so many ways by which we can communicate. This is thanks to the hard labour of past saints. They spent a tremendous amount of time and brought this knowledge for us to know and meditate with, in order to have spiritual success.

The way of communication is sound. It is not one sound but a number of sounds operating on each plane according to its vibrations. There is one sound that operates on all planes, from the god-head right down to this earth planet. Only a very few people have been successful in knowing the whole word. The majority of the religions express part of the word according to their experience. These are the sounds according to the distinctive planes.

There are so many other sounds as well on each plane. For example, each country in this world has its own local or folk sounds. Similarly, there are many rulers in each plane. If some aliens land in America, they will put forward the name of Mr Donald Trump. It will be said Mr Vladimir Putin in Russia. It all depends on the spiritual travellers' experience as a whole. You can be the knower of whole truth or you just accept what has been written or said by someone. *Lok* means universe or plane.

1. Physical world: The crash of thunder
2. Astral plane: The roaring of the sea
3. Causal plane: The tinkling of brass bells
4. Mental plane: Running water
5. Etheric plane: The buzzing of bees
6. Soul plane: Flute
7. Alakh-Lok: Wind
8. Alaya-Lok: Humming sound
9. Hakikat-Lok: A thousand violins
10. Agam-Lok: Woodwinds
11. Anami-Lok: Whirlpool
12. God worlds: Hhaaioommee
13. God world: Hum
14. God world: Hum means total silence.

If we add all these sounds together, then it becomes one distinctive sound that will represent all the planes, from here to the God worlds. If a person chants these combined sounds properly, he or she can have the experience on any plane or can manage to raise his or her vibrations to the desired plane or into "beingness" state. Over the millennia, only part of the "word" has been chanted. The saints have only managed to catch part of the word according to their spiritual knowingness.

For those saints who've managed to be almost in the presence of God, the sound is a straightforward "hum or total silence". If we travel into the worlds of duality, the word is *Om* or *Aum*. It is mainly used in Hinduism, and the people who meditate on this word are able to gain enlightenment or Krishna consciousness. The word *Aum* carries very powerful vibrations if "attention minus effort" is applied at the spiritual eye with full focus and chanted in rhythm.

It can raise the vibrations very high to the desired plane or to meet the Master, which can open up the inner experience and enable the Master to see the brilliant light or hear the inner sound. As I mentioned, there is one complete word that covers all the planes. It will suit everyone to have the full benefit. It will help to maintain a very high state of consciousness all of the time. It is known as "Haiome". To chant it properly, it will be pronounced as "Hhaaioommee". While chanting, the voice or sound should be raised in this manner:

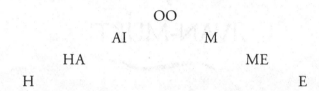

```
                OO
        AI              M
    HA                      ME
H                               E
```

For the first half up to *OO*, the word is chanted by vocals and half of *OO* followed by *M*, *ME*, *E* is a humming sound. Chant this for an hour and then quit. This is, overall, the highest vibration carrier word. This will cover every plane in existence, from the physical to the God worlds.

If part of the word is being used, as mentioned earlier, the experience will be partial too. It does not matter what word we use, it must be chanted with full focus and in a melodious manner, as if you are calling to someone you love. To materialise any success, it must be practised on a regular basis. As they say, practise makes perfect. Once you master the rhythm of the word, then chant it a few times to raise the vibrations and open up the experience.

Hhaaioommee.

JIVAN-MUKTI

Jivan-Mukti is one of the most common words used today by Indian-orientated religious followers. It means "spiritual freedom" from this world. It is the goal of every Seeker to make this present life the last one in this world and not to come back again to have another incarnation. It is very easy to say this, but to free one's self from this world is not that easy.

I have noticed the majority of people who use these words are fed up or are going through various hardships in life. It is their wish not to come back in this world to face the same situation again and again. There are very few people, who have earned good karma in their previous lives and are ready to leave this world forever. These people feel the urge within to seek a way to free themselves. As we are seeking a way out of this world, we become spiritual Seekers.

Spiritual Seeker

As spiritual Seekers, to materialise our goal, we have to find a spiritual path or a teacher who can lead us into the kingdom of heaven. To free ourselves from this world is a great responsibility. We follow a spiritual Master who can teach us, or we educate ourselves on how to free ourselves from the bondage of this world. I have also noticed that, after setting up this goal, we often fail in our attempt. The reason for this is that we cannot live up to the expectations that are required to materialise this goal.

I have also noticed that those people who are or were "failing in life" use these words, *spiritual freedom*, emotionally. They do not have the capability to execute their goal and materialise it in reality. We will not discuss karma in detail here, as it has been discussed in our previous book *The Way to God*. Good karma plays a significant role in this. If we do not have good karma, then it is not possible to liberate ourselves from this wheel of eighty-four.

Apart from good karma, we have to work on various other aspects related to this freedom. These are the five passions of mind—lust, anger, greed, attachment, and vanity. All these aspects have to be worked on or balanced out to run our lives as smoothly as possible. With this balance we won't act in any extreme way, which is responsible for creating bad karmas. As long as you are creating serious or nasty karma, you will never achieve spiritual freedom.

There is a very serious condition, which many people ignore or do not wish to follow. You have to set free every single person or thing within your circle before you can even dream of achieving spiritual freedom for yourself. This is where we fail. We do want spiritual freedom, but we do not wish to let go of our loved ones. It's the attachment that keeps us grounded. As I have said many times, all the relationships we have with people, such as mum, dad, son, daughter, and all others, are attached to us by karma.

Kal will create situations, where we will create more karma and get more tangled in this karma theory. Once you have balanced your karma, you will notice that you don't really have any serious relationship with anyone apart from surface communication. It is just to get along on a daily basis. Once you have reached this state of thinking, you will notice some kind of irritating or uneasiness within. This is the first indication within and you feel compelled to find a way to get out of this world.

You will notice that you don't really have any attachment to your loved ones or property. You have the capability of leaving all this behind at any time, without any notice or hard feelings. If you think or feel that you cannot leave certain things or habits, then just forget about your goal of spiritual freedom. If you cannot manage to let go of a few habits or things, then it will be a very big thing to leave your loved ones. They are more attached to you than anything else.

Spiritual freedom is a challenge to oneself to achieve in this life. It is more difficult than any other work or achievement. You may not realise it, but this is the sum total of all responsibilities put together and beyond. There comes a time in our lives when we realise, where we stand in our present life and we become spiritual Seekers. Now the question is this: Are we really spiritual freedom Seekers? Or are we making this search emotionally because we are going through some bad patch in life?

Is it possible that we want to get away from a situation or that, perhaps, someone has talked us into it and our emotions are playing up? I will say that, if overall your life is running smooth and you are feeling some kind of nudge within yourself, then I think it's about time to make a move. All religions claim to provide freedom from this world if you follow them. When you come to investigate, you will find that they are run by a certain system and are designed to improve social welfare.

These are the traps set by the Kal power to entangle you more in its booby traps, from which there is no way out. It is the same with the majority of spiritual Masters, who are claiming to be spiritual liberators. Actually, many are money grabbers, or in other words, pseudo-masters. And you will notice they are running their systems very successfully because you let them. It is a good salesman's pitch that makes them successful.

The majority of real Masters are silent or hardly known to many. Any religious teaching, when it comes to a commercial level, will always lose its spiritual touch. It requires a triad combination to achieve spiritual freedom—the right teachings, the genuine Master, and a true Seeker. If any one of these is weak, then nothing is going to materialise. In my opinion, it does not matter how good the teachings or the Masters are if you cannot free the others who are within your circle.

Then it is not possible to achieve Jivan-Mukti, as you have failed to pass the basic requirements. It is not a game or a toy to play with. It will take sheer effort. And freeing yourself from the bondage of karma is a huge responsibility. That bondage may have been built up over hundreds and thousands of lives. These karmas will not disperse as easily as we think. If a person is serious and sincere and puts in all the required effort, then it can be achieved within a very short period.

If any person reads *The Way to God* and adopts the qualities required, then I want to know who or what is stopping you from achieving your goal in this life. A person of this status becomes the spiritual knower and is free to leave the lower worlds at will and at any time he or she wishes.

This is Jivan-Mukti in reality.

MY LAST LAUGH

When I was born and I cried, others laughed and celebrated my birth. Everyone tried to pick me up and gave me love, kisses, and cuddles. But I felt that I was in a strange land. I was helpless to do anything. But others provided for me when I cried. At my suffering, others felt joy. When I was nurtured, I fell asleep. It was peaceful. This was my golden period. At least I had the chance to relive my old memories. Many times, I smiled, and my mum thought I was in communication with Spirit. Right she was.

It was the best way to pass time. Who wants to lie in a boring cot and act like a toy for others? They had fun, and I was in pain lying on my back most of the time. Many pulled my tiny fingers, but no one understood my pain. It did not take long for me to learn that I had landed in a world of struggle. Being so young, I had to establish my relationships. My mind could not yet understand who I was. They thought I was only a child, but in time it was revealed that I was the oldest of all.

They all sang the lullabies and laughed, but it was not my language. I knew I was in a strange land. They told me who I am now, but I knew I had been someone else before. I know that I am soul, but they gave me a very strange name. I thought, *Well, maybe that is who I am.* One time, I was Hindu. Next, I was Muslim. Then I was Sikh. Now again I was in a strange land. They had fun, but I was confused. Time went by and my old memories began to fade.

My new name began to seem familiar. I was enticed away from my true identity. A curtain came over my past memories, and I began to feel at home in this strange land. Once, the moon and stars were so close. Now they seemed far, far away. Still I had no fear. I played with a cat and a dog. They bestowed their pure love upon me. With their fur, I felt I was in heaven. Still I wondered, '*Who am I and who are they?* I felt love from all God's creation.

So far, it was my golden period. I felt that I was wanted. Before my birth, my mum had cried with pain. After, she'd cried with joy. And now, she cried when I am sick. Where I come from, everyone is happy and is in bliss state all of the time. After this knowingness, I felt that I was in a strange land. Would I ever know who I was and where I was? One day the answer came from Kal. "Welcome Home," said Kal. "I am your lord. May your journey be worthwhile."

In this world, I had a big account to settle. My legs trembled with the load, "Would I ever pay back what I owed? Now it is time to decide. Am I a man or a mouse? If I am a man, I had to face the challenge and settle my account. If I am a mouse, I could go with the flock and have a who-cares attitude. I knew within that, to face the challenge is a straight line, and the sooner I finished this line, just like an athlete, the sooner the game would be over.

If I followed the flock, it would be a never-ending circle. The challenge was strange and hard to follow, and people might laugh. The second choice is easy. As they say, if you can't beat them, join them. And you are welcomed in the family. You are happy and so are the others. Now I became the slave of five passions. I began to feel the pain; the emotions; the anger, lust, and greed; and the ego. Now I was lost in this strange land.

Now this is my home and my family, and I am attached to everything with an attachment more adherent than glue. Now who wants to leave this world? At the word *Jivan-Mukti*, I laughed. My youth appeared, and I felt that I was the hero and strongest of all. My five friend "passions"—came into play to give a helping hand. I knew I was not alone. With them, lots of other friends came. I thought this was fun. My marriage took place and turned into a fun fair, and emotions were high.

I felt on top of the world. Love, lust, and attachments were sky-high. I wished this would carry on forever. My karma knocked on my door, and a little voice said, "I am coming to see you." I was delighted to know that a new guest was coming. It did not take long. "Now it's party time." The new guest said, "I did not come for the party. We have an account to settle." The demands were made, and I began to pay this guest back. I was giving, and the guest was receiving, and I felt the pain.

Yet there was pleasure within this pain. Love, greed, and attachment all clouded my mind. All this taught me a lot, and I became the wise man. Now, in this world, I was the knower and philosopher of all—the dictator and big boss of all. And yet, I was in pain. I learned how to cry every moment, and I forgot how to laugh. Sometimes I laughed, but I felt that it was another joke. A single tear of my child made me weep, and a big ocean came out of my eyes.

A slight temperature of my child made me feel that I was going to have a heart attack. My child fell on the floor, and I rushed to the hospital. I felt my brain was going to explode. Yet I survived. I began to protect my child, my family, and my belongings. I was a prisoner within these walls. I began to think *I am lost in this wonderland.* I was within this maze; all the paths seemed familiar. Any paths or roads I followed led me back to the centre point where I had been before. I was tired.

I gave up and said to myself, "Who cares?" And I went to sleep. I was tired of this rat race and began to analyse within myself. *Who am I? And what I am doing in this wonderland?* The man of men appeared and said, **"I am the way, and the way is within**. Do you want to know the way? Come and follow me." After all these years, I felt peace and bliss within, and I remembered that I had felt this before.

He replied, "Yes, when you were with me last time. I sent you here to experience, but you were reluctant to leave and suffered at your own choice. Now you have realised you are in the wrong place. But now you are in the present moment, and it always has been. To me, it is now. But to you, it is a million years. Let us begin in this nowness, and soon you will be in this present moment, in happy everlasting bliss. Attachment intervened.

Emotions garbled within. Lust came, and ego came, along with anger. They all cried, and I cried along with them. I thought we were born to cry. The whole world was crying. The question came from within: *Will I ever laugh?* The God man appeared and smiled. I looked at his blissful face and felt peace within.

"Come and follow me. I will show you the way."

I felt joy. At last someone had come to the rescue. He raised his hand. I heard the sound and saw the light in my body and began to float above the ground. In his presence, for the first time, I felt I was not part of this world. This is just a glimpse; you can know more. Meditate and may the blessings be. I was over the moon. I was the same child again. The Master led me like a little child, and he showed me all the places where I had been before.

The Master's love was so great I wanted to remain a child forever. He gave me a nudge to grow up but I ignored. I thought time was on my side. I was part of the big tree, but as a leaf, my colour began to turn yellow, and my roots began to shake. I began to tremble with fear of losing my ground. I knew that my time was close. Fear intervened, and no loved ones wanted to help but waited for the leaf to drop. The ones I loved, thought it was fun.

Now I was wondering if there was time. The Master appeared, smiled, and said, "I am beyond time. You can be too." I begin to meditate. Lots of hurdles came. The mind began to act like a monkey. All the friends of mind, the five passions, came to congratulate the mind in its success. I was meditating but with the help of my mind, I was travelling to India and Japan. And without realising, I became a globetrotter. I was fighting with my loved ones, and I was boiling with anger.

I felt uneasy and quit. Master appeared again and said, "All these people are a helping hand to purify your thoughts. Give them love and let them be, and they will disappear in no time." I began to realise the grudges I was holding against them. It was not they who were holding me back; it was my own creation. The creatures of my own creation were fighting within, and I became the battleground. At times, I was a soldier and bandit. At the same time, I was a thief and a crook.

A vision appeared. "I thought you were going to be a saint?"
I began to give love to all and felt at ease.

The Master appeared and said, "Show me your hands." He looked and said, "You need to work more." I knew I had crossed the first hurdle, but there were many more to go. I meditated, but nothing came as easily as I had thought it would. When the Master was helping, I had become a spoilt child. Now I realised I had to earn for myself. The Master appeared and said, "I meditated for thousands of years to be where I am now. Never give up. I am always with you. You will succeed."

I meditated, and people thought I was insane. I have seen the light and heard the sound. And at the threshold, the Master was waiting for me. I felt like a little child again. The Master extended his hand, and we travelled above the shores. My effort was fruitful, and I became the traveller. People came to see what I had, but it was beyond their reach. To them, I was the wise old man. I knew that my time was near, though, and they all cried. I had my last laugh, and I proceeded to join '**Thee**'.

To all, may the blessings be.

SILENCE THE MIND

This is one of the main problems of all Seekers. As we approach our spiritual exercise, "meditation", we take all necessary precautions to have any spiritual experience internally and externally. We prepare ourselves for this. But as soon as we begin to chant the spiritual word, our sitting does not bear any fruits from our endeavour. Our mind becomes active and begins to wander around in all directions. After half an hour, nothing materialises, and we get up, unsatisfied.

The same routine follows for weeks, months, and years. Many people even blame the teachings or the Master, and they begin to drift off and seek elsewhere. This is not the solution, as you have failed to achieve anything. I have mentioned one condition in many places. The Seeker has to raise his or her vibrations up to the level of sun and moon worlds. Once you have achieved that, only then can it become the responsibility of the Master to lead you further.

The Master can lead you into the inner worlds in no time as soon as you sit down for meditation. But this way, the Seeker learns nothing. This way, you will be dependent on the Master all of the time, very similar to a child who cries for little things from the mother and seeks attention. Eventually, with time, we grow up and move on with our lives as adults. Similarly, if we want to become Master of our universe, we need to grow up with our own efforts and find new ways to silence this wandering mind.

There is always a solution to every problem. Our mind has the capability of thinking about more than one subject at a time. Actually, it can think about three/four subjects at any time. As we have experienced during our spiritual exercise, when we are chanting the word, our mind begins to roam freely at a far distance, without it even coming to our notice. By the time we realise it has been wandering, it's almost time to get up. This is where the half hour time limit fails you. It is recommended to meditate for at least one hour.

I have found a very simple solution to calm down this part of the mind. Once we calm down into a singular direction of thought, only then can we proceed to "deep *samadhi*" or to the level of sun and moon worlds, Asta-dal-Kanwal. Since we followed all the procedures for our practise of meditation, such as our sitting position and breathing to feel relaxed and calm, we begin to chant our "spiritual word". The word is chanted in a lengthy manner. For example '*Paramatma*' becomes:

Pppaaarrraaammmaaatttmmmaaa

As you can see, it takes a number of seconds—time—to chant this word.

To silence the wandering thoughts during this period, we are going to make good use of the wandering part of the mind too. This time, as you begin to chant the spiritual word, you will use another word to eliminate any wandering thoughts. Now you will be chanting two words at the same time, you have the capability of doing this. One word will be chanted verbally as normal and the second word will be silent. For example:

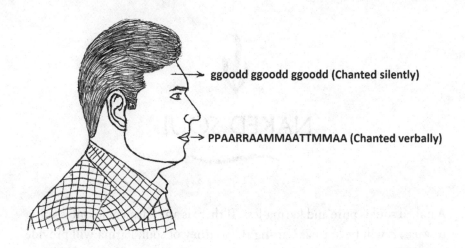

ggoodd ggoodd ggoodd (Chanted silently)

PPAARRAAMMAATTMMAA (Chanted verbally)

The second word can be any word of your choice, as long as it is spiritual. Examples could include *God*, your Master's name, or *Aum*. With this, you have silenced the wandering thoughts and made use of the capability of the mind to wander in a positive manner. You will notice very shortly that you have gone into an experience without any effort. Once you have made this a habit, your every sitting will have become successful. After a while, you won't even have to follow this procedure, as you will have trained your mind to stay silent. Good luck!

NAKED SOUL

A naked soul is pure and karma-less. If there is any garment a soul is going to wear, it will be karma. During the journey of soul, karma will provide two purposes—experience and load—which will keep it in the lower worlds until it manages to free itself, with the help of the Master. Soul has to work off all karmas that have been created and be as pure as it was in the beginning. The only difference this time will be the experience it has gained so as to become assistant with God.

This is the journey of soul as it leaves its creator in a nameless plane, an ocean of love and mercy, it was part of yet inexperienced. Then soul comes down to the soul plane that becomes its house while it is pure. But it cannot remain there, as it has no experience to become assistant within the God worlds. Under the guidance of Satnam Ji, soul enters the lower worlds, where soul becomes the responsibility of Lord Brahma.

Lord Brahma makes sure soul receives the proper schooling and returns as assistant to one of the lords, or Satnam Ji, or to the higher worlds. In the worlds of Brahma, soul picks up the etheric and mental bodies. Then soul is guided to the causal plane, where it picks up the causal body and eventually it is taken to the astral plane. There it picks up the astral body and becomes the responsibility of Dharam-Raj. Dharam-Raj becomes responsible for your physical journey, and he decides where to place you in the lower forms of life on the physical.

Soul is placed within the cosmic sea of life. Soul is given some karma known as Adi or prime karma and may be placed on the physical like a little worm on the ground or a little fish in the sea. Once you have been picked up as a worm by a bird or eaten by a big fish in the sea, your karma with others is established. You have just entered the reincarnation system. For many lifetimes, it does not bother soul. You eat, and in return you are eaten.

This situation is very similar to a small child; if a child has a physical ailment, the parents, under the guidance of a doctor, decide what treatment should be given to the child. The child is not aware, what is taking place, so it does not bother the child as much. Once we are grown up, the fear builds up, and we become more conscious of our pains. Soul comes to a point on the physical level where it leads a more active life. In danger, you are able to run or fly to save yourself.

You are also hunting others who are more vulnerable than you, and the wheel of eighty-four is in full swing. You enter the animal kingdom, and it becomes more of a struggle to survive. You cannot fly away, but you have to face the music, as the saying goes. You run away or fight for your survival. Some are unfortunate. They are caught by humans, chained, and become pet animals. Here, soul has no choice but to listen to the dictates of humans.

This is your life where you serve the humans with your good virtues, for example as a cow to provide milk or as a horse for them to ride on and in many other ways. This is the point where you serve, and the torture of humans puts good karma in your account, and you progress to human form. This is the first life form where you come to know that you are living some kind of life and what you can do for yourself and others.

Although you are not that clever yet for many lifetimes, it is this participation that adds experience to the soul. It is soul's maturity, and we become aware of our "I" factor in life. This I factor makes you aware of who you are, as a person among others. You could be a believer or non-believer in God. After many lives, your spiritual mind wakes up to the spiritual call within and you become a religious person. This is another web to tie you down to the physical ground.

You are very in favour of the religion you follow, and other religions seem a threat or almost enemies to you. It is not your fault. As a child, you are willing to follow any dictates from your elders or from the clergy in temples. They always seem to express religious thoughts to those who attend. But at the same time, the message is not to get involved with other religions, by labelling them as false religions. Our religion is the only one that can give salvation or freedom from this world, the ecclesiastical leaders preach.

And we as followers begin to believe this and express this to our children, and they become believers of the same, and this goes on forever. This is all part of the wheel of eighty-four. This is the entanglement created by the Kal for your benefit to give you proper experience. You become a proper extremist in one particular religion, and that is the only way to learn the full influence of that religion. Each religion teaches different aspects of life, and then you move on.

Each religion and each race of people will have an impact on soul as an experience. I have been part of all religions and races of people. With my experience, Hindus say, the only way out of this world is through their deities, which are numerous. So, you don't know which one to follow. The majority of people are not aware that all these deities are only within the lower worlds. The highest point they can reach is my old friend called Brahma, so 'What will be their peak point?

It still is part of the lower planes. We can achieve Buddha, Krishna, or Christ consciousness, but we are still within the lower worlds. All of these religions have failed to express at what point soul will have true salvation or Jivan-Mukti. All these religions are busy in social welfares. The needs and demands of the people are physically based. Soul and its welfares are not discussed, and no one wants to know why or learn more.

On the surface, many express that they are religious, but with thorough examination, you will come to know they are totally physical. How can they lead others to achieve Jivan-Mukti? Christians believe salvation is only through Jesus Christ. I wish that it were true. They believe that Jesus took the sins of this world on him and died on the Cross. Actually, he was the victim of the circumstances of that time and had no choice but to go on the Cross. He did not choose to go on the Cross himself.

He was sentenced to be crucified on the Cross. There is not now, nor has there ever been, nor will there ever be, a single soul in this world who is capable of taking the karma load of this world. This false statement has been made by many Masters in the past and will continue in the future. These people do not realise this is a violation of spiritual law, as it is untrue. If this were allowed, then there would be no need for the karmic theory and schooling for the soul.

Many times, with our spiritual success, we are given the opportunity to serve God in some minor spiritual position, and we misuse our authority and make false statements. We have to withstand the accounts of these statements and pay accordingly. As you may have noticed in my writings that I respect Jesus very much. So, it is my belief: I don't think, Jesus had said this himself. The ninth Sikh guru, Sri Teg Bahadur, who was alive during the reign of the Mughal Empire went to Delhi "willingly" on 24 November 1675.

To be assassinated by the king in order to save the Hindu religion and human rights as a whole. He never claimed that he was taking the sins of this world. He took this as "The Will of God". Later, his son Guru Gobind Singh turned the teachings into, what we know today as Sikhism. He asked all Sikhs to wear the Five Ks. All of these Ks are physical symbols. If you follow the teachings thoroughly and do good karma, you can attain Jivan-Mukti.

Islam has its own beliefs. Islamists bury their dead because they believe that, after death, one day in the future, all these people will wake up. If you look thoroughly into this belief, I don't think that practices of Islam are even aware of or interested in spiritual freedom. I am not giving this information to condemn any religion. As I said before, I have been part of all these religions, and I love them all very dearly.

My point is that they all show claim their religious domain as "the only way", when the truth is, none of them are; they have not come to the point of universal thinking. Once you have been through all of these religions, you will hold a universal thought—*I am an individual.* You will begin to search for a way out of this world. Once you are ready, the Master of the time appears and teaches you how to eliminate all karmas and remove all of the shackles that are holding you down.

Apart from God and its divine light and sound and the Master of the time, all else is illusion. It is designed by the Brahma to keep you grounded. Nothing in this world is a waste. All serves the purpose of training of soul. The most precious thing or relationship that we value most is the hardest to get rid of. You will be surprised to learn that the majority of the people in this world are attached to one word, *mother,* and the rest of them are attached to *money, status, my country,* and *my religion.*

As long as you are connected with any of these things deeply, you are not free. To all the saints, these relations have no significant value. You must brush off all traits; religious beliefs; thoughts; and, above all, the causal, mental, and etheric bodies simultaneously. We cannot take any valuables, near and dear ones, or religious symbols with us on our journey. Once we are cremated, all the religious garments or symbols we wear turn into ashes.

It does not matter what prayers have been performed or what physical temple you have been taken to. None of them can help. All it matters is how much good karma is in your account. *Good karma*—these sound like very favourable words. You cannot shake them or all the lower bodies off as long as the word *karma* is attached to your soul, unless you are a saint. Saints are only born to create good karma and to take on the karma of others, to free them of their pains.

Brahma is only doing its duty and makes sure you pass through his territory as a pure or naked soul. Consider the last line in my book *The Way to God,* in a chapter called "God-Realisation". It reads, "In my terminology, you have to walk even over yourself."

That is total karma-lessness.

REFLECTION IN THE MIRROR

In this discourse, I want to know the progress of all our little gods. I am sure you must have been at peace within. Now you know, all the moans and groans are not worth it. You must face the situations that come your way in a calm and balanced way. When you are calm, only then can you resolve a situation, as only then can you look at it with a clear mind. With blurred vision, you will not get the full details of the picture, and your judgement will not be correct.

Once you get a clear picture of a problem, then it does not take long to work it out. Staying in balance and positive is very important. Only then can you help others. The bigger the problem, the calmer you should be. Any person with a hot temper cannot think straight or think of others. At this moment, you are a problem too. All these discourses are eye-openers for you to realise how spiritually awakened you are. This discourse is to indicate where you stand on the spiritual ladder.

Now, after practising our new spiritual exercise, "I am God for today", I am sure you must have come to some realisation and made some effort in many ways to be like your creator. The more virtues of God you can adopt, the nearer you will feel to it. I am sure that you must have discovered something new about yourself, when previously you had a different view. Maybe this is the first time you have stood in front of the mirror to see the true picture.

Did you ever notice your face in the mirror? Your face looks the way you want to see it. But the truth is, if you look at your face from the viewpoint of the mirror, it is not the same. Your left eye or left ear is not the same; now it has become the right eye and right ear. To have any success, you must blend the picture on both sides, external and from within the mirror, and create a balanced picture that is very similar to your creator.

Now I will give you an example of how balanced, fair, and neutral we are. In reality, we are always far away from balanced, fair, and neutral. I was watching the TV this morning and the presenter was praising an actor who had success in his career. The actor replied, "I am always worried that, where I am today, if I don't work hard, someone else will take my place." In other words, this actor is so attached to stardom that he is not willing to leave the platform. It's the name and fame equal to attachment.

Whatever we do in life, it should be done on neutral grounds or for the good of the whole, so it will benefit you and, at the same time, benefit others. We build up this fear of losing our ground within; this fear is our failure point. It leads us away from God, and yet we are praying to God to give us success. This fear within does not want anyone else to take "our" place. This is where acts of jealousy come in. If you are doing your work with full honesty and within your rights, then no one can take your means away from you.

I am waiting for all of you to take my place, and so does God too welcome you as assistants. *The Way of God* discourse was to make you aware that you are soul. Once you become aware that you are soul, then it's not the soul that does not want to travel; it's your unwanted burdens that are holding it down to the ground. You can have Self-Realisation, if your soul is free or if it at-least is able to breathe freely. I know that most of you are or were Soul-Realised initiates.

Now the question is, Are you? My big problem always has been to hold myself to the physical level, if possible. During the spiritual chants, this was my main problem. I would sing the word for a few times, and I would be far away. Despite my efforts, soul always defeated me. I remember one time I was out of the body twelve times within thirty minutes, and all the experiences I had were on different subjects.

What is Self- or God-Realisation? It is the realisation of God's qualities.

The next question is, how **many** have you adopted? The more God qualities you adopt, the more God-Realised you are. Otherwise, you know my blunt answer. It's not the soul that doesn't want to travel; it is you who have trapped the soul. Most of you have used these teachings just to solve your personal or family problems. Any religion or teaching that tells followers, "Come to us, and all your problems will be solved," is misleading you and deceiving you as to your purpose in life.

If you cannot manage to solve self-created problems, then when are you going to have Self-Realisation? I hope, after reading this, you will ask yourself a question: Where do I stand spiritually? I am sure you know the answer. You must begin to act like your creator or at least act like your guru, who is a living example to you. I went to attend someone's funeral. He was a friend and nice person. His son, while paying tribute to his father, prepared a little speech.

His son made the remark, "If I adopt half the qualities of my father, then I will take it as I have been successful in my life." If you adopt the same attitude and try to adopt **half** the qualities of your creator, then you can definitely call yourself successful! The living Master of the time can give Self- or God-Realisation instantly, provided the Seeker is ready. All previous Masters and myself are providing or have provided all the tools to accomplish your goal.

There is nothing freer than soul, but you have trapped it so firmly; and it has become your failure point not to travel. I am not getting much response from our members in the neighbourhood. It seems like they are working so hard to be little gods. They don't have much time to make monthly report. The members living in Canada are always in touch. I have learned over the years that parents are the first gurus. Naturally, we are taught what they know. Some children are very lucky to have decent parents.

We learn very valuable points at a young age, and our life is successful. The point is this: Most parents are or are supposed to be our icons, but they are not our Bible. One day, I met a young man. He was shouting over the phone, when there was no need to do so. The situation he was dealing with could have been sorted out with a very calm attitude. When I asked him the reason he was shouting, the answer was, "Oh my mum does the same, and my dad talks loudly too."

Now the question was, have your parents' lives been successful? I knew them too. Their life as a couple had been almost hell. Therefore, they were not ideal parents. The young man must learn from their mistakes and try to lead a better and more peaceful life. I asked this young man to explore his parents' behaviour further. "Why were they shouting all the time?" I asked. I was told that this was the only way to get your point across.

So, to win the argument was very important. "My mum always made sure that the point has been made," he told me. Some people never learn. To them, it does not matter, even if these arguments destroy their lives. If the young man's parents had both moved away from the situation silently, it could have been good for the whole, for both parties. These are stubborn people who do not let the Spirit penetrate so as to solve the problem. Valuable lives are put at risk.

At what cost? One day, they will know, and it will be too late to regret. The chapter will be closed for both parties. These mistakes can create suffering for many generations to follow. We must watch our behaviour and what we say in the presence of our children. They pick up on our strategies and behaviours and attitudes naturally, and their lives will be moulded around the situations we present to them. I remember once an old lady advised me about my recent marriage.

"As a couple, you will never argue, fight, or misbehave in the presence of your children. They will also learn these habits." Teach your children the value of love and responsibility, and their lives will be successful. The majority of the time, we are responsible for the failure of our children in life, as they are reflections of our thoughts and actions. Those children who find their own ways in life with good karmas lead their lives successfully and become the pioneers of the way forward for others too.

Paul Ji taught three main points of speech to his wife, "Gail Ji". Before you utter a single word, pause for a second and think about the statement you are going to make. Is it true, is it polite, and is it necessary to say? If you apply these principles in life, your life will be wonderful to live as created by our creator. We make our lives miserable with our own wrong or irresponsible actions. Then we are praying to Spirit and saying many times during the day, "I leave this in the hands of Spirit." Do you?

I don't have any problems, when in effect there are more problems knocking at my door every day than there are for most of you. The reason I say I don't have any problems is that, when a problem is standing at my doorstep, I say to it, "Hold on there. You are not allowed to step in." As, I said previously, do not let the Kal circle around you. It is very important to do your spiritual exercise. After a successful session, you will feel the flow of Spirit all day within yourself.

That will reflect in your countenance that you are full of love, peaceful, and in balance. When you are living in the bliss state, lots of negative situations will come and bounce off without even touching you. A physical example would be that you don't find many cockroaches living in a clean house. If you prefer, you may live with them. That is your choice. Long ago I invited someone to check the grammar of my writings because I was feeling a bit rusty in this field, and that person kept rephrasing a majority of the sentences.

I said to the person, "I want to keep my writing as original as possible. So please, only check spellings and part grammar." But a beautiful conversation took place out of our laughter. This person was having lots of up and downs in life at that time. I said to the person, "Do you know what? You love to rephrase my writings. Why don't you rephrase your life?" This person was dumbstruck and at a loss for words. Finally, he said, "Oh my God. I never thought of that!" This person took my advice, and now he is very happy.

We all can do the same, as this lifespan is too short. We must make the most of it. We must adopt the qualities of God as I suggested in the last few discourses. By these principles you will come to know how wonderful this life is. There is so much to achieve or to unfold, as Paul Ji said many times, that there is always a plus element. It does not matter what you have achieved so far. There is much more to know yet. Some people who are very close to me make the same remark.

"There is no way we can do as much you have done or achieved in life." I say to them, "You are joking." I have so much more to do, and I am always on the move. Or as they say in English, I am always on my toes. You may think the same, but this is true. There is no end to the purity. You must carry on until the day you are sitting within the heart of God. That will be your day of celebration. But on that day, you will not celebrate, even if someone asks you to celebrate. You will ask yourself, what is celebration?

Now you will be living in the virtues of your creator, a peaceful bliss state. The five passions will be balanced. Anger will be under control. There will be no reaction to the emotions, as is true of God watching us all day—when we try to create chaos every moment of the day and all through the world. God is not affected by our doings. and yet it takes all our doings upon itself at the same time. If you understand this philosophy, then there is nothing else to understand. Now do you know who you are?

You are the reflection of God.

FRUIT

What will be the fruit of our relationship with God? When I was young, I used to admire one special mango tree in our village. It had a majestic height, it was not easy to climb, and it had green leaves on very healthy branches. Out of these branches, a number of small green mangoes used to appear. With season and time, they grew in size but were still green. The weather changed the colour of mangoes to yellow, but the fruit was still hanging on the tree.

With maturity and the consent of God, it left the branch and fell on the floor (physical) to be served. Now it was in service as assistant. Nowadays, we don't have the patience to grow our own fruit on the branches of Spirit. Every person is looking for shortcuts, and all our problems are the result of these shortcuts. We can go to the market stall and buy the fruit. That is the easy way out. But to grow your own and then eat it, is an experience in itself.

When we try to find the easy way out, it means that we have created the wall within us, as we are not a part of God. As long as you are asking, it simply means you are not part of God. As long as the wall is there, it simply means no success. Demolish this wall and hang onto the branches of God tree as a part of itself. All your problems will vanish! I can only provide the tools. You have to make the effort. Spirit can help in every corner of your life, but then you end up doing nothing and we will not achieve our goal:

Be the reflection of God.

THE PROPHETS OF GOD

The prophets of God are great "souls" and are especially sent to earth for a purpose. Their births are always forecasted prior to their arrival in this world. These souls are very close to God or known as assistants. God does not or will not invest this power in any individual, religion, or prophet to make the statement that this person is the last prophet. This kind of statement is good enough for self-pleasing or to brainwash the followers. This kind of statement is used when any religion is feeling a threat from other religions on the basis of domination.

Every person loves his or her religion, whatever it may be. A very similar situation can be found on Mother or Fathers' Day each year. To draw the overall picture, you will notice that some parents are excellent, while others are average, and many are below average. But consider these two days, and you will notice that majority of the parents get the same message. On the greeting cards: "You are the best mum or dad in the world." Are they really? Maybe not, but in the opinion of their children, they are.

This is because we fail to look outside and make comparison. Despite this, we still want to believe "my mum and dad are the best". Every person has the right to express his or her opinion. We have no right to change someone's mind. That would be a violation of spiritual law, better known as psychic space. All the religions in this world today had a prophet in the beginning of the religion. Otherwise, new religion would not materialise in this world. Many times, prophets do appear time after time in some religions.

Noah, Abraham, Moses, Jesus Christ, and Muhammad are the descendants of Adam and Eve. This is how they are connected and are historical figures. Sri Ram, Krishna, Mahatma Buddha, and Guru Nanak have the background of Brahma, Vishnu, and Shiva or better known as figures of Hinduism. The descendants of Adam and Eve and Hinduism do not believe that they are connected to each other, though they are. There is only one God, and every person is created by this supreme power. We are connected to each other as souls and are part of it.

Adam and Eve

The birth of Adam and Eve was in 4000 BC according to biblical scholars. Adam and Eve are the origin of Christianity, Islam, and Judaism. It may not be true, but according to the mythology of Christians and Muslims, these were the first two people created by God. The birth dates are approximate. If this was the case, these are the signs of late Bronze-Age, instead of the Golden-Age as believed originally. Considering the dates of Adam and Eve, it does not add up in time.

If they were the first two people, surely their birth would have been long ago. Looking at some history provided by the biblical literature, we take the idea that Adam and Eve were born in 4000 BC—or 6,019 years ago. That indicates this is how old the civilisation of this world is. I am sure scholars can come up with better figures than these. The prophets like Abraham or Jesus must have told the age of civilisation somewhere. But sometimes followers don't pay attention to this kind of information.

Noah

It is also believed by many that Noah appeared "ten generations" after Adam and Eve. Noah was born in 2940 BC approximately, as the timing of floods on the earth was in 2,340 BC. At that time, he was 600 years old. Noah received the prophecy and was guided to build an ark (a ship). Apart from his family or loved ones, he was also guided to take a number of animals on board.

Whoever boarded the ark survived, and the rest were wiped out due to their wrongdoings—in other words, being the channel of evil spirits. The rain flooded the earth for 150 days. Eventually, the ark came to rest on the mountains of Ararat in Turkey. Noah led his family and animals to the Promised Land, and later he died in 1990 BC at the age of 950 years.

Abraham

Abraham was born in 2052 BC. The place of his birth is known as Ur of the Chaldees, Iraq. He is best known as the patriarch of Judaism, Islam, and Christianity. He was married to Keturah. He died at the age of 175 years and was buried in the cave called Hebron. He has been known as the father to many nations. Abraham was a descendent of Noah's son Shem. It is believed that Jesus and Mohammad are the descendants of Abraham. Abraham has been accepted as a prophet by many religions as well.

Moses

Moses was born in 1540 BC and translated from this world on 1420 BC. There was a prophecy regarding the "deliverer" to free the slaves. This was the prophet Moses. He survived death at birth. To save the young Moses, his mother put him in a basket and left him in the river in the hands of his destiny—which he was to fulfil, as he was raised as a prince. Later he was discovered—that he was the deliverer—and he was ordered to go into the desert with little food, to live or die. He survived and became a shepherd. And one day, he went into the presence of the Lord.

Spirit manifested as burning bush, and Moses received the spiritual powers he needed to fulfil his destiny. He came back to the pharaoh and told him to free his people, but he was refused. After many struggles and curses, the king gave up and agreed to free the Hebrews from slavery. Moses prepared his people to leave and led them to the Promised Land. When they reached the Red Sea, Moses managed to prepare the passage with the help of Spirit—an event known as, "the parting of the Red Sea". As the people were crossing, the king's army arrived for a revenge attack.

As the army entered the Red Sea, it closed back up, and a majority of the army drowned. On the way to the Promised Land, Moses went to Mount Sinai to meditate and for future guidance. He was given the Ten Commandments. During his absence, the people began to worship evil spirits or pagan gods. Moses got angry and put things right. After that, he passed his spiritual mantle to Joshua and asked him to lead his people to the Promised Land. Moses retired into the mountains and finally died at the age of 120 years.

Jesus Christ

It may not be true, but Jesus Christ is said to have been born on 25 December 0000 in Bethlehem. As for his mother, it's known that she was virgin. He was born in a stable. According to the myth, angels were present at his birth, and three wise men made a visit on camels to see the young Jesus. His birth is known as the arrival of the Messiah. Which had taken place according to the prophecy, and people were waiting for him. His real name was Yeshua Ben Josef. He was baptised by John the Baptist.

After that, he went into the wilderness as a test, where all attempts were made by Kal power to cause him to fail and prevent from completing his mission many times. This. Is known as the dark night of the soul. After forty days, Jesus Christ succeeded and appeared as the Messiah or the prophet to lead the world. This word *wilderness* does not mean a desert or jungle, as this experience can take place anywhere. It is the fight within. At that time Jesus was alone, so there is no record of what took place.

Only when you have been through this state of consciousness can you verify this statement. Jesus began his ministry. His early disciples were fishermen. As he got popular, he was a marked man, and many government ministers or religious leaders felt threatened. He made many statements relating to his kingdom of God. Although the message was on a spiritual basis, the leaders of government and religion began to find or plant false evidence against him.

During his short ministry, he healed many people and raised the dead, turned water into wine, and performed many more miracles. The religious leaders felt the threat and wished to get rid of him, any way they could. Jesus was making statements against them in public, and they found it humiliating. The Pharisees were always on the lookout to accuse him and get him killed. In the end, they managed to kill him by means of crucifixion. Jesus Christ is claimed by his followers to be the Son of God.

This is a great threat to any religious body even today, so be prepared to face the worst. This is why there are some very highly spiritually awakened people who keep their silence. We can forget about 2,000 years ago. Even today in the modern era, people are not ready to accept this kind of statement. Jesus gave the message of God to the best of his ability and went on the Cross to be crucified, as per the final decision of Pontius, the governor of Judea.

Due to his sacrifice, he is alive forever in the hearts of his followers. His body was kept in a tomb under the supervision of guards, and a large round stone was rolled in front to seal the entrance. After three days, the disciples found that the tomb was empty. The angel appeared and confirmed the resurrection of Christ to the disciples, and later Jesus appeared to them as well. It is not easy to spread the word of God. All prophets have the same message but appear in different parts of the world.

As it is the requirement of the time and for the majority of time, the consequences are the same too. The Bible was not written by Jesus Christ, but there is a contribution from Moses and many others. There is a great contribution from Saul, who was born Jewish but had a spiritual experience on the road to Damascus and changed himself to be a believer of Jesus. Later he was known as St Paul. He was also martyred around 67 CE.

Muhammad

Muhammad was born on 22 April 570 CE in Makkah, Saudi Arabia, and died on 8 June 632 CE. He spent most of his time in meditation on Mount Hira. One night (in 610 CE), he was meditating in the cave when an angel named Jibril visited him and told him to recite the name of Allah. Later he received spiritual revelations that were written down, and the holy book the Qur'an was assembled.

Muhammad began to believe he was chosen as the prophet of Allah. Once he started to gain popularity, the people of Makkah felt threatened. He took his followers to Medina in 622 CE. That journey is known as Hijrah, and the Islamic calendar began. It took him ten years to come back to Makkah, and a number of wars were fought including, the Battle of Badr, Uhad and Ahzab.

The term *jihad* is given. Finally, Muhammad was accepted as the prophet of Allah. Sharia law is a religious code of living that directs the individual to lead an honest and spiritual life. Muhammad married at the age of 25 years to a wealthy woman, who was 40 years of age. Her name was Khadijah. After she passed away, he married Aisha. He married a few times, and finally he translated from this world at the age of 62 years.

THE PROPHETS OF HINDUISM

We have discussed the descendants of Adam and Eve. This is the second line of descendancy that runs parallel to the theory of Adam and Eve. The figures and prophets discussed in this chapter were here long before Adam and Eve; their parallel theory is known as Hinduism. Their origins are from Brahma, Vishnu, and Shiva. They have been here since creation began in this physical universe. They were already residing in the upper regions of the lower planes.

All three were given the responsibility of looking after the well-being of souls while they were experiencing the lower worlds. This was to create physical bodies for souls and to maintain the well-being and destruction of the physical bodies at the end of their lifespan. Thus, the soul can have experience from another dimension. Brahma, Vishnu, and Shiva are better known as Creator, Preserver, and Destroyer. This is why the lower worlds are better known as the training ground for souls.

Shiva was established on the physical world for this purpose. There is evidence that Shiva is still here because he shows his presence to sincere followers now and then throughout this world. The historical moments of these three spiritual giants were lost during the times of the Golden-Age and the Silver-Age. Hinduism claims the trio has been here very recently, during the times of their prophets. The history of other religions is also very poor, as they cannot relate at all with these three spiritual giants.

Their spiritual writing is based more on the surface of the physical world than on the higher or spiritual worlds. They were not here only for

Hinduism; they were responsible for the whole of creation. They still are and will continue to be until the end of Kali-Yuga. Other religions may accept this statement or not, but this is true. The saints of Hinduism managed to look back into the past, as they were interested in the study of stars, sun, and moon relating to this world and the effects of this relationship.

We will discuss the study of planets in our "Physical Universe" chapter. The basic theory of Hinduism is excellent, but how it is expressed in movies is total mythology. These venues express that Hinduism has been here since the beginning of time, but its written history fails to go beyond ten thousand years. Therefore, 3,893,201 years of history is lost. So, we go by the number of years mentioned by their scholars.

Sri Ram

Prince Ram, the son of King Dashrath of Ayodhya, was born in 5114 BC. The story of Ramayana is the base of Ram's existence in this world. After Ram's marriage to Sita, he was about to be announced as the next king, but due to some conspiracy in the family, his father told him to go into exile for twelve years. At that time, he was about 25 years old. At this time in history, both India and Sri Lanka (Ceylon) were at full civilisation.

Sita was the daughter of King Janak of Mithila, now Bihar, India. At the same time, King Ravana was ruling in Sri Lanka. The population of these countries was in the hundreds of thousands at least. Ram is known as Maryada Parshotam (Obedient One). He taught the principles of obedience to his parents and to the entire civilisation. He was not an ordinary person. He was born with natural ability of spiritual powers.

During the period of exile, King Ravana abducted Sita due to some grudge regarding his sister. To free Sita, a big battle took place between the armies of Ram and Ravana. Hanuman (a monkey species) gave a helping hand to Ram during this period, and Ram was victorious. When Ram and Sita returned after fourteen years, people lit candles as a welcome gesture. Nowadays, that day is known as Diwali. It is celebrated every year all through the world.

Lord Krishna

According to legend, Lord Krishna was born without a sexual union but by mental transmission. Krishna was born in 3228 BC in the dungeons of a prison where his mother, Devaki, and father, Vasudeva, were kept by Devaki's brother King Kansa in Mathura, Uttar Pradesh, India. King Kansa was given the prophecy that one of Devaki's sons would kill and de-throne him and restore righteousness as a whole.

So, King Kansa imprisoned his sister and brother-in-law, and he killed every child of theirs at birth up to the sixth. Spirit or God tricked him during the birth of the seventh child, and now it was time for the prophet to be born. Near the time of Krishna's birth, his father became worried for his safety. Then, during a vision he saw that the guards would be sleeping and the prison gates would open themselves. At the time of his birth, Vasudeva put Krishna in an open basket and moved outside.

It was exactly as he had seen during the vision. He took his son to the house of a friend called Nanda, exchanged his son for Nanda's daughter of the same age, and came back to the prison. Nanda's wife Yashoda raised Krishna as her own in the village called Gokula. When Vasudeva was taking baby Krishna from prison to Gokula, according to myth, a heavy storm struck. During that storm, a serpent with many heads appeared and provided a cover over his head as a protection from the rain.

So, these were the signs of a born prophet. Later on, many attempts were made to kill Krishna, including poisoning. In his youth, Krishna returned to Mathura and killed Kansa who was his uncle 'mama' and returned the throne to Kansa's father, who had been imprisoned for a long time. Krishna became the leading prince in the kingdom. During those days, he became friends with Arjuna and his brothers (the Pandavas) who were his cousins.

Later there was a war between the Pandavas and their cousins the Kaurvas over the right to rule the kingdom. All negotiations by Krishna failed. Krishna did not want to take either side in the war, but both sides approached him. Finally, he offered that one side could take his whole army and the other side could have him. But he would not use any weapons.

Duryodhana tried to be cleverer and chose his whole army. The Pandavas chose Krishna, and he became the charioteer to Arjuna.

Upon arrival at the battlefield, when Arjuna saw the opposition, they were his cousins, grandfather, and other relations. He felt very uncomfortable to fight against or kill any of them. Finally, Arjuna put down his bow and arrows. Krishna gave him a discourse on physical and spiritual life to establish righteousness in the world and his duties. Later, these discourses of spiritual awakening were assembled as the *Bhagavad Gita*. Krishna was married to Rukmani.

In some literature, it is mentioned that he was married to 16,108 wives; out of those, 8 were his principal wives, and the rest were rescued to save their honour. During his last days on earth, Krishna returned into the jungles, and he was in meditation. A hunter named 'Jara' shot an arrow into his bare feet, as he mistook the glorious lotus shine under the feet for a deer's eye. Only a few prophets have the glorious lotus "Padam" under their feet, especially those who are sent by God directly to accomplish a mission.

Krishna ascended to heaven spiritually, and his death marked the end of the Bronze-Age and the beginning of the Iron-Age. Although he died at the age of 125 years in 18 February 3102, he never aged after his youth.

Mahatma Buddha

He was born in Nepal in 563 BC. He was born a prince called Siddhartha Gautama, and the king built three palaces for him to make sure that he would lead a happy and peaceful life. Legend says that, on his three visits outside the palaces, he witnessed sickness, old age, and death. He was disturbed by these experiences and wanted to achieve freedom from this. Despite being married and having a son called Rāhula, he walked off to find salvation or enlightenment at the age of 29 years.

He studied under the teachings of Alara Kalama and then moved on to study under Rama Putta. Still he was not satisfied and moved on to seek further. Later he followed the path of asceticism and performed heavy meditation with minimum food, a single leaf or a grain of rice. This did not work out spiritually, as he nearly starved to death, and he gave up on that idea. He made up his mind to meditate under the pipal tree until he received enlightenment.

After sitting for forty-nine days, he and his companions received enlightenment. At that time, he was 35 years old and taught the middle path for forty-five years. Before departing from this world, he was known to have thirty-two qualities or the signs of being a great holy man. By many, he was known as the ninth avatar of Lord Vishnu and is considered a prophet by many religions. Finally, he passed away in 483 BC at the age of 80 years.

Guru Nanak

Guru Nanak was born on 14 November 1469 and passed away on 22 September 1539 at the age of approximately 70 years. His birthplace, Nankana Sahib, is near Lahore in Pakistan. At his birth, the spiritual light was seen. Later on, a serpent was seen to provide a shadow over him as he was sleeping. Once it was noted, as he was sleeping under the tree, that the sun moved with time but the shadow remained on the same spot.

During his younger years, lots of divine qualities were noted. He made four *udasiya* (journeys). His last journey included visiting Makkah, Medina, Basra, and Bagdad. He was travelling to Kabul and Kandahar, and a number of miracles happened, which are recorded in Sikh history. Evidence, such as his handprint on a large stone that was thrown at him, is still available today. Now the temple where the stone is kept is known as Panja-Sahib (hand with five fingers).

Although by birth he was Hindu, as he was spreading the word of God, the Hindus were upset, but his spiritual message was on a universal basis. He taught that God is one and that Hindus and Muslims are the same in the eyes of God. One time, he was captured by King Babar (Islam) and then released when the king realised that this person was spiritually extraordinary. He was the first guru of Sikhism and wrote 947 hymns, comprising of Japji-Sahib.

In the beginning, he shed light on the one and only God as Ikonkar—God's first personification Satnam Ji and his qualities. I have not seen or heard this depth of explanation of reality anywhere else. In his last days, Guru Nanak returned to the place called Kartarpur and passed over his spiritual mantle to the second guru known as Angad Dev Ji. Finally, he passed away on 22 September 1539 to be in the presence of God.

RELIGIOUS TRACK RECORDS

To sum up all the theories, let's look into Christian theory and dates given by some Bible studies. These indicate that the origin of Adam and Eve at "4000 BC" is no more than 6019 years approximately. According to Hinduism, Lord Sri Ram was born in 5114 BC—7,133 years ago, and at the same time, it indicates that there was full civilisation.

Considering the number of people at that time, we can easily add another 3,000 years. That will make 7,133 plus 3,000, which comes to 10,133 years. At the same time, recorded history of ancient Egypt indicates there was full civilisation at 7000 BC. All the theories do not add up compared with the population of this world in the multi-billions. People have not dropped from the sky within this short period.

Having some spiritual knowledge, sometimes I feel that the scientists are far ahead compared to religions. At least they are mentioning the time scale in millions of years. The construction of this world can be a few million years, but civilisation of the humans living in this world, according to the beginning of the Golden-Age, it began 3,893,120 years ago:

Satya-Yuga	(Golden-Age)	1,728,000 years
Treta-Yuga	(Silver-Age)	1,296,000 years
Dwapara-Yuga	(Bronze-Age)	864,000 years.
Kali-Yuga	(Iron-Age)	5,120 years so far

The Kali-Yuga will continue to complete its cycle of 432,000 years and that will mark the end of civilisation for this time. I am not against any theory given by any religion but I always felt uncomfortable according to the visions I have seen a long time ago. My visions are very much in line with the *'Nakal'* (copy) records at the Katsupary Monastery in Tibet, where all the spiritual records are available. In my visions, the jungles of this world were in full bloom.

In other words, the world was ready to receive the human accommodation to provide food and shelter. I have seen the first five people landing on earth. It was in the jungles, as most of the world was jungle. They were in the upright position (standing). I saw them coming down to the ground feet first, and the Satya-Yuga began. So, I do not agree with the theory given by our scientists that we have progressed from the monkey species.

As the theory goes, during our early days, we were walking on our four feet, better known as two hands and two feet. If this was true, what is stopping the present monkey species from walking on two feet; it is much easier for them to copy humans. The monkey clan is one, and humans are another part of God's creation alongside other 840,000 of species. Each creation is individual to help soul's spiritual experience.

Nowadays, some scientists in this world are trying successfully to cross-breed some species. This is a violation of spiritual law and can lead to many upheavals in the future.

First five people arrived on earth were men. Females came or were created later, as agreed on by a few religions. I am aware of these five people from the last forty years when Darwin and I went back in time. I was surprised to learn about this last year when a friend gave me a book to read called *'Gurbani Katha Vichar'* by Iqbal Singh, which compares Hinduism to Sikhism. Singh writes that there is a mention of these five people in, 7000 years old Hindu book known as *Sri Shiv Puran*.

The Puranas' provide spiritual history. The evolution theory by Charles Darwin is very young comparatively. They were known as "Panch Sant Kumar" (Five Saint Princes), and they were very close to God. That is why they were especially chosen for this purpose to begin Satya-Yuga. The lifespan of these people was a few thousand years. So far, I have managed to trace one person out of these original five. He appeared on earth a number of times to perform spiritual duties.

He was seen in sixth century then again, he appeared in sixteenth and seventeenth century Asia, where he is part of history. He was born again in India in the eighteenth century and passed away in the middle of the nineteenth century. This is just to give a little hint to some curious minds. I can see that he has come back again and taken his spiritual duties for many years serving God. As you can see, these people operate on a universal level, so there is no question of "my country or yours" or "my religion or your religion".

There are many other active souls who have been here since the beginning of all these Yugas. They have made thousands of repeated journeys all through the world. These assistants of God are not allowed to sit still in a bliss state somewhere. There are billions of souls seeking spiritual help, so they will appear as directed by the Spirit. This is the original point of discussion regarding prophets. There is no such thing as, "This is the first prophet of this world," or, "This is the last prophet of this world."

The people who make such claims are false. This world is good enough for another four hundred thousand years for human habitation according to the 'Nakal' records. While some religions are less than 10,000 years old, they feel that they have the authority to forecast the future for 426,880 years. Over this span of time, thousands or more prophets are coming to accommodate the spiritual knowledge of the time. The prophets who, we are so proud of today will be totally forgotten, as we have forgotten the prophets who were here during the period of Satya or Treta-Yuga.

LOST HISTORY OF PROPHETS

I'll give you a few examples of how this history is lost. Jesus Christ was here only 2,000 years ago, and this religion has failed to produce his true looks in a picture. The image that you see nowadays is totally self-created and does not resemble his true looks. Let's take a look at the most recent religion of all, Sikhism, which is no more than 500 years old and has had most of the facilities to maintain every single detail of its history.

You will be surprised to learn that the Sikhs do not have a single true picture or a true sketch of their ten gurus. As I had the privilege to be in the presence of Guru Nanak, I am aware of his looks. Unfortunately, none of the pictures on the market today are any closer to his true personality. There is no sign of spiritual countenance on his face. Apart from his image, Guru Nanak has given us very valuable spiritual writings that have been changed in the past and are being changed at the present moment.

One day, this truth will be lost, as it will have lost its true power of continuity. The same will apply to all other religions as well. For as long as we can maintain the true contents of any spiritual writings, it will hold its spiritual powers. As soon as we try to dilute its true meanings, it will become thinner each day and will eventually disappear from the face of this planet. I'll give you another example of how the contents of writings are lost. Paul Ji brought the teachings into the open in 1965, "The Path of Enlightenment".

He said at one point in one of his cassettes, "My writings may be edited to sound better or more effective"—very similar to the Bible. But at no point did he say that you can add any more to his written words. I have this audio cassette for reference. Once we begin to alter, add, or subtract parts of written words, we lose history. The Kal, or negative power, set up the trap. The mind becomes its victim, and history keeps repeating itself.

This was the whole reason for writing the chapter, "Power" in *The Way to God*. I don't think people understand the value of originality. All paintings of famous artists sell in the range of millions of Dollars because they are original. It is the name and fame that leads to all the forbidden activities in spiritual law. Only the born Master or prophet is capable of keeping the teachings pure like they should be. He is the only one who will keep the teachings to God's expectations.

From other or routine Masters, you can expect anything. My writings are very simple, and they may not be up to the current standards of grammar. I do not wish my writings to be altered in any manner because I have said it the way I want to say or express it. *The Way to God* is my first book, so I gave it to someone to check the grammar and make a few corrections. After a few weeks when I received my book back, this person in question made remarks that it was done very professionally in line with today's reader.

I said thank you. Later, I wanted to see the improvements. When I read it, it sounded very foreign to my mind. I had to rewrite the whole book again. Now you see my point. The moment you do any alterations, it will lose its spiritual charge and will become similar to any ordinary writings. Civilisation will come to a near end many times within this next 426,880 years with the help of weapons of mass destruction. The next big disaster is expected at the end of 2029 or the beginning of 2030.

That can change, provided the vibrations of this world improve. At this moment Kali-Yuga is very young, and we have lot to learn. Prophets are born with spiritual knowingness. Not everyone can be a prophet, even if they try; prophets know their past, present, and future. The death philosophy regarding the age factor does not apply to them. They know exactly when they are going to leave this world. They can also delay their stay for longer if they wish, very similar to Sri Rebazar, or they can choose to leave early.

The lifespan, number of years or number of breaths a person is supposed to take in this or one lifespan, is not fixed, as mentioned in many spiritual scriptures. They are written to please the mind of humans because their tolerance level is very low if they lose a loved one. There is another statement that is not true but has been used to create fear in the mind so that a person can do as much meditation or good deeds—that is, to face death is truth at the end of a lifespan. Spiritual philosophy is different.

Death is no more than changing clothes for the soul, while to live is the ultimate truth—the way for soul to have experience. The more incarnations that soul goes through, the more experience is gained. Death is truth to the human body. And "to live" is truth for the soul. While you are aware of both situations, do not be too bothered with these two truths. Follow the middle path and gain as much experience as you possibly can.

Wherever you are sitting, you should know that you are the centre of the whole of creation. Spirit is flowing through you directly. You are the source of God to reach every soul in the universe. Your physical identity has dispersed into thin air. You are only aware of yourself as soul, and through your soul you are reaching everyone. If you know that you and God are one, then what is there that you cannot know? The prophets are in this position.

Not everyone can become a prophet, but you can work hard spiritually towards it through a number of lives. One day, you will appear as a prophet on this earth. God has created each soul with this ability, so do not underestimate yourself. Any person who underestimates his or her spiritual abilities will never succeed. Keep focussed on your goal. The statement "this is the last prophet" is not true. I know one religion that misleads its followers by saying that God has said this".

God does not exist for only one religion. When you know that all of the religions are man-made, you understand that they try to please their followers. Under the influence of such statements, it is very difficult for the new prophet to show any authority, as people do not wish to recognise them. A new prophet fails to speak because he knows that people are under this influence and will not accept him. So, one thing leads to another, while this newcomer could far superior to the previous prophets.

There is only one prophet who is the creator of all the prophets, and that is God itself. The prophets do not wish to call themselves prophets because they know what the truth is and who runs the show. It is only their followers who want to label their own saints as such, in order to have an edge over the other religions. Who are they to put a stop to any more coming of prophets? They claim that their religion is very strong, and it is on the surface. Internally, though, they are very weak.

The day that the prophets stop coming will be near the end of Kali-Yuga. The Yugas, such as Satya, Treta, Dwapara, and Kali-Yuga, at present, are a clear indication of the presence of humans on earth to tell us of their existence. Otherwise, the names of the Yugas are totally meaningless. This search will carry on, as we have lots to learn yet. Christians have done some research on many known saints, but their names only exist in mythological stories.

Research has proved that, in reality, they never existed. There are a number of Hindu stories based on mythology, whereas reality is totally different. So only believe what your inner being wants to believe. God has given you this knowingness. Keep working towards your goal, and one day, you could be the future prophet. To have any success, your mind should be very calm. Overactive or devious minds are misleading. Sincerity, patience, silence, and many other virtues of God will help you to materialise your goal.

I was in India very recently, and one day, about ten people came to see me. They were all very sincere but following other paths, and they all had some questions to ask. One young girl about the age of ten asked me, "Where is my third eye?" I said, "Do you really want to see it?" She said, "Yes." I asked her to come and sit on the chair near me and told her to close her eyes. I advised her what to do and where to look.

She followed the instructions very sincerely, and suddenly her third eye opened, and she saw the spiritual light. This is the proof of having a simple or uncomplicated mind. There was another lady. She was unable to concentrate on her spiritual eye while her mind was very active and wandering everywhere. She asked, "Is there any technique that can help for this problem?" I said, "Yes. There is always a solution to every problem."

I explained how to go about this situation, where and how to concentrate, and she found our "Silence the Mind" technique very successful. This technique is written earlier in this book. She tried this technique while we were all talking. Later, she remarked that she was totally isolated from our noise and had a spiritual experience. This proves how live our teachings are, while others are very passive paths. But people are still following them. I wish them success.

PAUL TWITCHELL

Paul Ji went through many struggles to bring the true teachings into the open, so that everyone could have access to the truth, as it had never been revealed. Or at least it hadn't previously been revealed as openly and in such a straightforward manner. The truth had always been here, but it was written in a certain style or contained hidden meanings. In other words, a simple mind could not grasp the message.

Due to this, people were walking away from traditional religions, as the answers to their questions were not given in a simple and straightforward language. Spirit chose Paul Ji for this task. It was a huge task for Paul Ji to run around the world and study all the religions of this world—to present a clear picture of spiritual truth on neutral grounds. By his doing so, whoever came in contact with these teachings would say, "These teachings are for me."

The task was huge, and the time allotted to uncover the whole truth was short. So, the struggle began. He mentions having seven teachers who were responsible for his spiritual growth. Rebazar was the last one to provide the final spiritual spark to hand over the spiritual mantle—in order to bring the teachings into the open in 1965. His ministry lasted just under six years till he passed away on 17 September 1971. His wife, Gail, was guided spiritually to present Darwin as the next Master at the worldwide seminar in October 1971.

A number of other Seekers had this experience too. Paul was born on 22 October 1909. Paul mentions Paducah being his hometown. According to the US census of 1910, which covers the area of Paducah, Kentucky, the records show that he was six months old. His elder sister, better known as Kay Dee, was about five years old at that time. I am sure this is why Paul Ji decided to hold the worldwide seminars on this date. It was necessary to come in line with other world religions and have a focal date for some kind of celebration.

Paul Ji did mention that the passing of the spiritual mantle took place on 22 October on a full moon and so on. Up until today, none of the changes of the spiritual mantle have taken place on this date. It is very important to put the record straight, as Paul himself passed away on 17 September 1971, aged 62 years. The spiritual mantle changed again on 17 October 1981 from Darwin to a new Master. Due to disputes, the spiritual mantle came back to Darwin on 12 January 1984.

This is why I have never agreed from day one that we can limit Spirit to any day, time, date, or place. Spirit is beyond these limitations. I mentioned this in my previous book as well. This was the reason Paul Ji mentioned in one of his taped lectures that most of his work would be edited in fifty years' time. There are some dates and statements that are contradictory. Most of the religions were jealous of his success. But for Paul Ji, it was a hard labour of love for Spirit.

As a result of this jealousy, he was poisoned in Spain a year prior to his final passing. It was a great struggle for him to keep his body going until his successor was ready to take over. The poison given to him caused a lot of damage and injury to the internal organs. At the end, his face was almost white, as there was no blood in his body. People were surprised how he managed to carry his body. Finally, he passed away of heart failure in Cincinnati in the presence of Dr Bluth, the president of the organisation and Paul Ji's personal doctor too.

Dr Bluth was also expecting the spiritual mantle after Paul. As he was not announced as Paul Ji's successor at the seminar in October 1971, he left the teachings. When this change of spiritual mantle takes place, there are (and will be in the future) those who are not happy and will leave. This is very natural. We cannot dictate to Spirit what to do. Once we understand this, then we will be the winners. It also has been admitted by some members of the family that Paul Ji was born out of wedlock and later adopted by his father.

This was revealed to Paul by his grandmother after he graduated from high school. This upset him for a while. Paul worked as a journalist for a number of years because he loved to write. This was why he managed to write a good number of books in his lifetime. He had this spiritual urge within to come out and touch everyone's heart. And people felt that what he said or wrote—the teachings—were for them. This spiritual urge within and the system he was living in made him feel trapped, as though some physical obstacles were in his way.

This was why he gave himself the name "Cliff-hanger". He held onto the spiritual thought that was beyond human grasp, so he created his own world. Someone made the remarks that Paul Ji was a liar and a crook. These are the people who never knew who Paul was. The position Paul Ji held as a child or youth, no friends or family members could have understood. Neither could they understand what his mission was or what he was doing.

For example, I am one of four brothers; my three brothers will never have a clue who I am. I do not share with them what I have been up to or done over the years spiritually. If one of them started to spread negative rumours about me, all I could say was, "He doesn't even have a clue who I am." Day to day, we live on a normal basis just like any human being, and at the same time, we live in our own world. Both my worlds run parallel to each other and both are justified in their own ways.

No one will ever know what is going on. Normal humans may not even understand what I am talking about here. All these years, I have kept my high times as well as my struggles to myself. Spirit teaches you not to utter a single word until you are told to do so. I will give you another example. I have been married for forty years, and my wife never had a clue about my spiritual training—because I kept everything to myself until my goal materialised on the physical level.

As the saying goes, I have drunk the whole ocean and the person standing next to me wouldn't have a clue that I have done that. The ocean is very small compared to all the universes. The training is so intense. Now you may understand what is meant by "golden silence". In early March 2008, I had no choice but to reveal myself and who I am to my wife and to two very close friends. Now I can talk about and understand what Paul Ji might have gone through.

Some people believe that Paul Ji invented the entire line of Masters. This is not true; I have met most of them, apart from one or two. As I mentioned earlier, it is always better to be honest right from the beginning. So far, I have not met Master Sudar Singh of Allahabad. This may be because I simply did not require any experience under his supervision. It is said that Paul gathered certain words from other religions. I believe that this is true.

He chose these words to give his teachings universal touch; otherwise, they would be known as an extension of some other religion. Paul Ji joined the navy in 1942 and served till 1945. Some of us are not aware that Paul was married before in September 1942 and was divorced from this lady in 1960. She was also interested in spirituality, and both of them joined some religious teachings together. She mentions that Paul was always in meditation.

He met Gail Anderson in 1962 and married her in 1964. As Paul was a super reader, he met Gail in a library where she used to work part-time, and she was fascinated by his underlining remarks on returning of the books. He was taking an average of ten books on a daily basis, and all of them carried Paul's remarks. Paul Ji was beyond imagination. Although Paul Ji had such tremendous knowledge, he was a very shy person. It was Gail who told him to do something with his knowledge.

At the same time, he was receiving inner nudges from Spirit to bring the teachings into the open. This finally materialised in 1965. Paul Ji was asking Spirit, "Why me?" During that time, he was also writing letters to Gail on a daily or weekly basis. This was to educate her about what he knew. Later, these letters were published as a book. Paul Ji came in contact with a number of religious teachers. One was Meher Baba.

Paul also joined the ashram of Swami Premananda in 1950 and left the ashram in 1955 due to some trouble within the group. Later, Paul joined the Dianetics and Scientology movement, based on the teachings of Ron Hubbard. He did not stay there for too long, although he did become one of the consultants within that group. Paul Ji joined the Radha Soami group in the mid-fifties, and he was initiated by Saint Kirpal Singh.

They had a good relationship until 1963/64. Gail was also initiated by Kirpal Singh in 1963. Paul wrote one book in the late fifties and gave it to Kirpal Singh to publish for him in 1963. But he did not agree with the way Paul had expressed this truth in his writings. After that, their relationship was not healthy, and connection between them was broken. Later, Paul asked for his book back and published it himself in 1967. It is quite obvious. It happens now and then.

The founder of Radha Soami, Shiv Dayal Singh had the same problem back in the mid1800s, as he could not share himself and what he knew with anyone else. So, he started his own path. During the fifteenth century, Guru Nanak did not agree with Hinduism, though he was Hindu himself. At present, his teachings are known as Sikhism. This is why Paul Ji brought new teachings into the open in 1965 as himself, and Radha Soami did not agree on certain semantics.

So, it was inevitable that they would break their ties. All the teachers Paul Ji had been with contributed to his spiritual education in one way or the other, but they were not very sympathetic to his teachings. Paul Ji had found a connection to the spiritual truth, which they never had or did not like. Finally, it was Rebazar who gave Paul Ji the finishing spiritual touch, and he was now ready to teach. People have tried to understand Paul Ji, but they have failed.

To understand Paul, you have to be like Paul. If your approach is physical or material, you will never know who he was, other than to admire his writings. Paul himself was a great researcher and made every possible effort so he could bring the teachings into the open. This is the failure point of Seekers nowadays. They don't do any research and rely more or less on the words of Master. That is good indeed, but if you put a bit of effort into your part and research, you will learn more and will eventually become the master of your own universe.

You will create your own vision of reality. Paul Ji said, "Don't believe what I say. You only believe when you see the reality for yourself." Paul Ji mentions that it took him fifteen years of intense training to hold the spiritual mantle. Paul Ji never claimed that his spiritual mantle came from Radha Soami. He learned what he required and moved on to his final training under the supervision of Rebazar.

In the same way, my background is from Nanak Sar "Sikhism", but I received the final spiritual spark from Darwin. Some American people claim that Paul Ji imagined the character known as Rebazar. That no such person actually exists or has existed. These are the people who have no spiritual insight and cannot stand others' success. Although Paul Ji is not with us physically, these people are welcome to walk through my door any time to read my diary.

There, I have recorded any number of my experiences with this spiritual giant. Again, it is up to them to believe; otherwise, no convincing will be enough. There is a claim by some people that Paul Ji has plagiarised part of his writings from other writers, such as Julian P. Johnson. They have produced the evidence from *The Far Country*. At the time of writing this book, there was no such law as plagiarism, or it was not taken very seriously and it was common practise among writers.

I want to make a point here that there is not a single religion that did not copy from another. There are similarities between the Bible of Christianity, the Qur'an of Islam, and the *Bhagavad Gita* and Guru Granth of Sikhism. There is no such thing as the original, as writers are always influenced by someone else's work. I don't think that anyone wants to copy others. I think during your studies, the influence of what you have learnt is printed in your subconscious.

When you try to write on the same subject, it may look or appear similar to someone else's writing. Rebazar regularly visited Paul to teach him all the knowledge he required to take responsibility for bringing the teachings into the open. The training is so intense that many times you get fed up with it and ask the Master, "For God's sake, do I have to go through this?" The Master shows no mercy until you are conquered by Spirit and surrender to it.

Although the Masters have unfolded beyond our conception, when you take birth on the physical level, refreshing training will be given. The Master of the time will put you through all the physical activities and problems that are not even in your way. This is so that, as a Master, you will have experienced and know all the problems. This will enable you to guide and assist the people who approach you with their problems. Paul Ji was one of the best spiritual travellers of his time.

The Master is only used as an instrument by the Spirit to get the message out. Physical personality worship has no place in the teachings. Paul said he didn't want anyone to ever put him on a pedestal. We never forget the human self, but we have to rise above it. This is why I keep repeating myself, that I am no better or higher than any one of you; but no one wants to listen or believe. This is because of the sincere love they hold for the Master.

At the same time, there are those who will focus on, ridicule, or criticise him. This is nothing new. Ridicule of the Master has always existed and will carry on. This is so in all walks of life. Those who challenge or question try to compare the Master with others through their mental faculties and try to bring the God-man to their level. The spark of God is within each soul. This is how it communicates with each form of life. In the same way, God has invested its similar power within the Master of the time.

On that basis, each soul is connected to the spiritual soul of the Master. Any soul that is ready can make the contact. Do not expect the physical Master to be aware of all situations. Paul started to write discourses for his first three students, and these amounted to thousands in three years. In the early days, Paul Ji started the teachings under the name of bilocation in 1965 but soon realised it sounded more or less like astral travel. Then he adopted the name of E.........., when he was based in San Diego, California, 92113.

He started a business. This does not mean he wanted to run a business. It means he was willing to pay tax on the money he received from his students. Paul was paying taxes, but he realised that, due to the war in Vietnam, most of American funds from the treasury were spent on weapons of destruction. He then decided to register the teachings as a charity. He also felt a lot of pressure from the tax sector, as there were too many aspects to deal with.

Paul Ji felt he was spending more time being a businessman than as a spiritual leader. This was not his intention. He made his living by his own means and had his own communication lingo. He was a hero in his own way. He created his own world of living. That's why he would say that he is living in this world but not a part of it. He was very shy and wanted to live a private life. But when the time comes, you cannot hide.

He taught us to grant freedom to any person and all religions and love for all life. He knew each person or religion is connected to God's plan with a golden thread. This is why he said, "Be yourself and let others be." Do not try to convince anyone to believe what we say. That Seeker who is more sceptical in the beginning later turns out to be a better believer. We should be ready to take any criticism and answer with honesty what we know.

Paul Ji wrote a book called *Difficulties of Becoming the living Master*. He mentions his difficulties and the struggle to bring the teachings into the open. He was more interested in the unfoldment of an individual soul to find its way back to the god-head as assistant. I am always thankful to him for the golden gift he has left for spiritual Seekers. You will always find people in all walks of life who never fail to criticise. Let them be as well.

DARWIN GROSS

Darwin received the spiritual mantle in October 1971 after Paul Ji passed from this world on 17 September 1971. Once, Paul Ji came and spoke to him in a Southern accent without showing his physical presence. Paul Ji gave him the message to join the organisation that he had not been aware of, and then his search about the teachings began. He enquired of people in his circle about this, and luckily, his sister found a book by Paul Ji and told him, "This may interest you."

It was a biography of Paul Ji, and as he touched the book, he felt a spiritual sensation in his physical body. After reading that book, he ran through most of the bookstores in his area for any more books on the same subject. Yes, he found some more, and immediately he wanted to enrol for discourses. Fubi Kants appeared to him as well, and Master Sato Kuraji was a regular visitor to him during most of his youth, as were Lai Tzes and Rebazar.

Physically, Darwin met Paul in October 1968 at the second worldwide seminar held at the International Hotel in Los Angeles. Finally, he met the man of his dreams, and Paul Ji gave him his mission to carry forward as the future living spiritual Master of the time. It was three years after joining that he became holder of the "spiritual power" for God. Do not be deceived by this physical time of three years. The Masters in this line are trained over many lifetimes.

The teachings he received during his childhood were very similar to those he learned when he met Paul Ji, so he felt at home. This is my personal experience. I joined in 1976, and in 1978, I was fully aware of my future assignment. And I had no doubt in my mind that I could do the job. You breathe and live this spiritual life naturally without mentioning a word to any soul. Darwin and Paul Ji were aware that time was very short—that the physical and spiritual training had to be accelerated.

Paul Ji was aware that his time to leave this world was nearing, and he had made this known to a close circle of his Seekers. Paul Ji gave the message to Gail to announce Darwin as the present living Master of the organisation. There were some other people who were also expecting the spiritual mantle in America, "who joined before Darwin", and someone in England too. Although Paul Ji had announced in his writings that the next God-man was fourteen years away.

He is in his teen years. Paul Ji could see that this next Master would not be ready during his physical lifespan. So, he proposed Darwin's name to the nine super souls, and they accepted. At the right time, they were responsible for taking him to the valley of Tirmir in Tibet, and he became the 972nd living Master. Earlier, Paul Ji had told him that his spiritual name was "Dapren". Or more famously, he is known as "Dar Ji".

At the fifth worldwide seminar in October 1971 at the Flamingo Hotel in Las Vegas, Nevada, Gail made the announcement, sharing Paul Ji's instructions that Darwin was the present living Master. She read an unpublished poem, "Golden Hour", by Paul Ji and presented Darwin with a blue carnation. Sri Darwin gave his first speech, and the love of Spirit was flowing everywhere, and the Seekers felt the joy.

Darwin was such a spiritual giant walking among us. We never felt him as a physical person or personality. I always felt as though Spirit was walking live everywhere. Once you looked at his face, it was very difficult to take your eyes off him. You could feel Spirit sitting right in front of you. It was not physical personality worship. Due to this flow of Spirit, people came in thousands to join the teachings. The flow of love we felt was totally phenomenal.

Everyone felt out of this world. Darwin was born on 3 January 1928 in North Dakota. His family background is Russian, and his great-grandfather moved to America. His parents were Christians. He was married in his younger years, but the marriage only lasted seven years. The pair separated from each other with mutual consent, and they had one son and a daughter. He joined the US Army at the age of 18.

When World War II was over, he was in the 492nd Screaming Eagles division of the United States 11th Airborne Division with the motto "The angels, hell from above". He was placed in Japan to serve. There he met an old Japanese Master. Sato Kuraji, he was his regular visitor to accompany him at lonely hours and to protect and guide. After leaving the US Army, Darwin studied electronics engineering. He worked in that field and managed to create some inventions.

Since his childhood, music had been the love of his life. There was a piano within the household, and he also learned to play "Vibes". During his master-ship, he managed to produce a number of songs and musical cassettes. He performed at most of the seminars, and the Seekers felt blessed. He also managed to perform with known American musicians. He has written a number of books and discourses, and he travelled with Paul Ji to many countries.

I love his book *From Heaven to the Prairie*, in which he revealed very important information to the true Seekers. Darwin experienced many physical body problems since 1961. With bad luck, he managed to damage most of his body parts. He had a long history of back problems, and a number of discs were removed. The muscles under his shoulder blade were painful from time to time. Both of his kneecaps had been operated on, and the heavy structure of his body was not very helpful.

During one European seminar in England, he needed to come down from the stage to meet the Seekers on the floor level. I was standing next to him to assist, along with another Seeker. I knew that he would not manage to make his way down the stairs. He put his hand over my shoulder for assistance. I said to Darwin, "You can put all the weight on my body, and I will manage." He replied, "I know you can." The other Seeker said the same to Darwin, but he looked into my eyes and said to the other Seeker, "No.

He has already taken my weight." Only I knew at that time what he meant. It is possible the other Seeker may have been thinking of physical weight, when Darwin was hinting at spiritual weight. Darwin had a heart of gold. He was the ocean of love and mercy. At the request of any Seeker, he would take the Seeker's pain and suffering on himself, and he suffered. He wanted to see that his Seekers did not suffer but progress spiritually as much as possible.

I noticed that the Seekers adopted a habit of throwing every little bit of pain in Darwin's pocket without bothering to investigate or ask themselves, are we doing the right thing?

Darwin did his part as a Master as well as a friend. Now the question is, have we progressed spiritually? I don't see that we have. We became too lenient on the Master and failed to become the masters of our own universes. Some are fighting at the drop of a hat as the saying goes, and others are crying over little things.

They can easily manage to fill up the ocean with their tears. A great man's effort has been wasted. In the last three to four years of his life, Darwin suffered from poor eyesight. He lived on heavy prescribed drugs to keep the pain away. Did any Seeker offered to take his pain? No! We were too busy in our little huts. And still we are busy doing the same tasks, which are useless and worthless. Under the direction of Darwin, the spiritual growth of Seekers and of the organisation was booming.

A large number of Seekers were joining throughout the world. Three major seminars were held every year: The worldwide seminar, the European seminar, and the youth conference. Darwin loved children very much, as they are an expression of Spirit. The flow of Spirit was so good that, during the seminars, people felt as though they were floating above the ground instead of walking. The shake of a hand or the Master's gaze said it all.

One attendance at any seminar was good enough to collect spiritual food for the year. The Master released more spiritual food than the Seekers could digest. This was the advantage point for the Seekers, if they could have taken advantage of this flow and progressed spiritually. Instead of taking this advantage, they got more involved in praising the Master—which he deserved very rightfully. But they failed to gain any proper core spiritual ground for themselves.

Today, they could have claimed, "I have done this for myself!" Darwin provided every possible experience for the Seekers without much effort on their part. All the Seekers had to do was hold good vibrations and a positive attitude. This was the cause of too much leniency on the Master and laziness on our part to do practically anything. Now, how many students are here who can claim, "Yes, I have mastered this in my life"? Not many—apart from one or two—so the average is very low.

I believe there is still time to do something worthwhile. During that time, there were some people in the office who were followers but still held some grudge in the background over Darwin having become the Master. Two years after becoming the Master, Darwin married Gail on 13 October 1973 in Sedona, Arizona, and their wedding was announced at the seventh worldwide seminar. The applause was thunderous. The general consensus was, "What took them so long?"

Some took this as a negative point marrying his master's widow. Gail acted as his secretary during their travels for seminars because she had gained a tremendous amount of experience working with Paul. This marriage did not last long. In 1978, they divorced each other, as their ways in life went in different directions. They remained friends. Then, Darwin married a third time in London. This marriage took place in London as well as in Hawaii.

But again, the marriage was short, this one lasting only a few months. Later it was declared as if it never happened. I don't think that this marriage phenomenon was suited to Darwin because the demand from Spirit was so huge. He had to put physical relations to the side and moved on to fulfil the commitments he had made to Spirit. After that, Bernadine Burlin, better known as BB, became his secretary and remained so until her last day in this world.

She was a great support to him, and out of this sincerity she wrote a book about Darwin entitled *Hero*. The other person who supported and stood by him all through the ups and downs was Mr Bob Brant. He was the original manager of the organisation. He walked out with Darwin when Darwin was removed from the office. This was where Darwin failed to consult Spirit: Who could be the actual candidate that Paul Ji had mentioned?

Later, a few other things were also done that were out of place within the guidelines of the teachings. In Sedona, two flags were raised—one with the "E.. symbol" and the other, the flag of the United States of America. There were a number of other things too that were approached or dealt with on the physical level, when they were supposed to be dealt with at the spiritual level only—nothing else. Paul Ji designed this teaching not as a religion but beyond religion.

Now let's consider the questions raised by the flying of the US flag. Is this some kind of a political party? Is this teaching totally based in the United States? Later, Darwin and the new leader could not get along. Once this happened, it became a catastrophic situation within this organisation. Something happened that had never happened in spiritual history. This was a dark day for Spirit. There must have been something between them that led to this kind of situation.

As they say, it takes two hands to clap. Some known Seekers in the England said, "We smell something from Darwin's picture." Up until today, I have all the published material from 1981, 1982, and 1983. Many photographs of the "new leader", but I smell nothing. We must learn to respect all souls. Sometimes I wonder if people who made these remarks have learned anything from the teachings provided by Paul Ji. They have learned nothing as far as I am concerned.

The "new leader" had done nothing wrong directly to me. I take the situation as it was—the decision of Darwin under any circumstances. The new leader claimed that, in March 1980, Darwin paid him a visit in the camera department at Menlo Park Office. Darwin told the new leader his plans, saying he wanted to step aside as living Master and asking if he would accept the position as his successor. They both agreed. (See Eckankar Trivia, 1980).

There is no doubt that Darwin did pass over the spiritual mantle to the new Master on 17 October 1981. A formal announcement was made, and a blue carnation was given to him, a very similar approach to that made by Gail in 1971 (which doesn't have any spiritual significance). A number of physical agreements were made to secure the future of the organisation. The new leader was to take over the office and Darwin was to retire on a good pension.

It did not take very long for things to go out of proportion, and the rest is quarrelsome history. I myself went on neutral ground. I did not take sides. I knew the two of them had created the situation, so I would let them sort it out between themselves. Afterwards, due to lots of wrongful physical activities, Spirit did not accept the situation. It had to intervene through the known Masters, Fubi Kants, Yabal Sakabi, and Rebazar Ji.

I am a witness to this, as it was a spiritually based experience. According to my diary it was decided on 9 January but changed on 12 January 1984. The spiritual power was given back to Darwin. This is totally a spiritual based experience; no one can prove or challenge it. During one of the European seminars held in England, Darwin admitted that he had chosen the wrong person. I was witness and heard him say this. In addition, it is in written statements in many places.

Once a decision is made, it is always very difficult, almost impossible, to rectify. Later, through lawsuits, Darwin was forced to stop using copyrighted logos of the organisation—the organisation he had been "head" of and that was owned by him by rightful means. As the Masters say, all the lower worlds are illusion. Therefore, everything is possible. Darwin made a fresh start under the name Sounds of Soul, which later turned into Atom: Ancient Teachings of the Masters.

By making some copyrights, you do not own the world. I suggested to Darwin, "We are not short of vocabulary. Any words you will use will become spiritually charged, as you are the Master of the time." Now again, I have not been recognised by the Atom organisation, and I have lost all of the words that he used. It does not bother me a bit. I am not short of vocabulary. I can create words myself any time I require. Darwin had taken the karmas of so many and suffered in his body.

In return, even those Seekers whose suffering he had taken on, walked out on him. Darwin had no access to the organisation's communication structures to the membership, so he lost his contact with the majority of them. Our teachings are here to assist and give our goodwill to any soul throughout the world—to those who want to experience God worlds in this life. We do not condemn the Seeker in such a way that he or she falls into the traps of negative force.

Darwin only managed to gather a few of his followers by making personal appearances in England and visiting a few near and dear ones in the United States. After all these years, I wonder about those Seekers who left Darwin. Have they learned anything or progressed spiritually? Only they know. Any follower should remain wherever he or she is happy; that is the Seeker's chosen destiny, and it is his or her psychic space. We on the physical level do not run these universes.

God is running the whole show. All we are doing is participating in its will. Darwin moved on in life to spread the message of God to the best of his ability, without caring much about his physical health. I have never seen him feeling down. He was the true picture of Spirit, as God had made him especially to be that. As they say, these Masters of the time always have a special spark in their eyes. They are also known as "eagle-eye Adepts".

All the Masters have special facial expressions, as God has made them with its own spiritual hands. They express the flow of spiritual love for all to feel love and bliss. With Darwin, there was no shortage of that. Darwin suffered from every angle you can possibly think of. He came to see me to say a final goodbye just before leaving his physical body. I shared this information with some close members at that time.

He translated on Saturday 8 March 2008 at 10.35 a.m. Pacific Standard Time US. In accordance with his wishes, no service was held. On 12 March 2008, his physical body was cremated, and the ashes were dispersed in the Pacific Ocean at Gleneden Beach on the Oregon Coast. Shortly afterwards, there were four seagulls forming a square. It was Darwin and three other Masters mentioned in the next paragraph, overlooking the spot where the ashes had been placed until the ashes were swept away.

It was Darwin himself and the three other known Masters who approached me on 15 March 2008 to give me the consent to carry forward the spiritual torch until destined. Sri Darwin will be missed in the physical by all; but he will live forever in our memories. Darwin, we all love you and thank you for what you have provided for us.

SHER GILL

As I have written about Darwin and Paul Ji, it's about time to complete the lineage. I will mention myself to let people know of my background and to share my struggle leading up to this master-ship, to come to the point where I am today. It has been a long struggle, which I will take, as the saying goes, as "the will of God". I am aware of my previous lives. Darwin and I went through them together a number of times.

I have been a very active contributor to spiritual services throughout history under the instructions of God. Some of my previous lives are written about in my private diary. It will be published soon, and the title will be *The Will of God*. In brief, I was here in the beginning of this physical world and came on a special mission to establish humans at the beginning of Satya-Yuga. This world was especially designed for the occupancy of humans, as well as other species such as birds and animals.

As I mentioned in *The Way to God*, food and caves were provided for shelter. This all came out of my personal experiences. I was here during the struggles of the Christian era. And then I played a very active part during the times of prophet Mohammad. I then moved on to the fifteenth and sixteenth century during the struggles of Sikhism, where I have an outstanding name in history. I don't have any attachment to these names. Otherwise, pride would come in and halt spiritual progress.

We are only doing our jobs or missions allocated by Spirit; the doer is God itself. This was one of the reasons Guru Nanak appeared to me when I was nine years old. As you notice, I have moved from one religion to another. Hinduism is another one. Many followers, especially Sikhs, when they are discussing with me, are only interested or feel better if their past-lives experience is within Sikhism. That is very limited thinking because Sikhism is only 543 years old.

So, what were they doing before that? We must adopt a universal approach as a soul in order to progress spiritually. This was why I have mentioned in my book that all the religions are connected to me in one way or the other—as they all are part of my journey. This is why I am in the position I am in today, as a universal soul. I don't see any point in holding a debate with any religion to compare. There is no comparison, as all of them are doing super jobs for the souls.

We must move on, as we don't believe in taking a rest. So, I was told again to come back in 1953. Under the command of God, we can come and leave this world without a trace. That means no attachment to any names or family. We pick up a new physical identity every time and begin with the mission and leave everything behind. Once my present lifespan ends, I don't want anyone to remember me. This time, I was sent on a special mission, which has been interrupted by some people.

Because of this, I could not spread the word of God the way it should have been done. It has been a great loss to many true Seekers, and to some extent, my present journey has been wasted. When I was very young, my grandmother revealed that a very famous saint, Baba Nand Singh of Nanak Sar, had forecasted my birth. So, at a very early age, I knew what my mission in this life would be. I definitely knew that my life would be lived on a spiritual basis.

I came to England on 8 October 1967, as my father was already living in London. I had no intention to come here, but being a child, I could not refuse. I thought Nanak Sar was my future home, but destiny had something different in store for me. I received a forecast at that temple for the future, and Baba Isher Singh still visits me now and then, and I enjoy his company. I had learned spiritual discipline and detachment because Baba Ji's theory was mainly based on these two principles.

So, by joining any organisation you do not become a Master. Mastership comes through the spiritual contribution made over many lifetimes; only then can Spirit establish you at a certain place, from where you will continue in this position. Here are some interesting instances in my life, before joining Darwin:

1. My birth was forecasted by a saint.
2. My mother used to tell me that I did not speak verbally to anyone until I was six years of age, but I could communicate with sign language. Many people thought I was born mute.
3. I saved a child's life by looking at him.
4. I had an experience of invisibility and many more miracles.
5. When I was 9 years old, Guru Nanak appeared to me all night long.
6. I had a rude awakening; I call this a rude awakening because it took me almost forty years to realise what had taken place when I was young.

This is what I was talking about during the chapter on Paul Ji, when I said the Masters are born with these miraculous powers. Later, I will give you some hints. So, this is what I was talking about. We are born with these abilities. I learned to stay silent since I was young. That is the best way. Otherwise, people begin to crowd around you. At the age of twenty, I was searching for my spiritual goal. Finally, at the age of 22, on 26 September 1976, I joined "The Way to God" under the supervision of Darwin.

In 1978, it was revealed to me, that I was to be the next person to take over the responsibility of master-ship. I was not surprised. And some of my past lives were also revealed. That is what leads me up to today. I began to work even harder, because most of the nights I was in the waking state and meditating. As I said before, I have slept on the floor most of my life. I remember one day Darwin appeared and said to me, "You don't have to work this hard." He was aware of my past lives.

This was in early October 1982. I was not feeling well spiritually, as I thought that I was wasting my time in this world. I requested that Spirit

Sher Gill

excuse me from my given mission so that I could move forward with the next mission. This was to leave my physical body purposely at the will of God. This was why I felt that my life had been wasted—no better than a vegetable life. It was at that time that Satnam Ji appeared and told me that he had to take the physical form to investigate.

"What has happened to my son". That was an instant revival to my spiritual life. I was told to move on with my life and prepare myself to be ready for 1985 or, at the latest, 1986. During that time, Paul Ji took over my final training because I was a little upset now and then with Darwin, although we had a tremendous love for each other. As I said, our relationship was like that of a father and a son. So, I was executing my rights over him spiritually.

I remember one day when Paul Ji appeared in an angry mood, when Darwin was standing right next to me. He said to Darwin; "Can't you even manage to train this one person?" Those were his exact words. And he added, "From now on, I will take over!" Those days, I was behaving stubbornly with Darwin because of the position he had put me in. It was 5 December 1983 when Rebazar Tarz came to see me. We had long conversation about the master-ship.

At the end, he told me, "Your time is coming in two years, so be prepared." Then he left. However, 1985 and then 1986 came and went. Nothing materialised because Darwin was put in a very awkward position by the organisation, so on a physical level, he was helpless to take any action. Probably he was trying to establish some physical grounds, but nothing was materialising. Meanwhile Fubi Kants and other Masters paid visits to me to keep my spirits high.

After too many dates and promises, I said to myself on 23 March 2001, "Call it a day and forget the whole thing." I decided to lead a normal life like anyone else. Considering my age at that time, I thought that a chance should be given to a younger person. I forwarded my request to Spirit and Darwin—that is, to find someone else—and mentally, I started to plan my retirement. First Paul Ji came and spent some time with me. He said that "he" (Darwin) couldn't find anyone else.

At that time, I realised there was quite a shortage of trained people with this state of consciousness. It also made me wonder what happened to those eighty-five people who were under his training. Once during a European seminar, he made the statement that there were eighty-five people under his training for master-ship. I was sitting in the audience and listening. I knew it was not true. Sometimes, he used to make these kinds of baseless statements.

One hour later, Darwin came, looked at me, and said, "Now it's time." Then many other conversations took place. Time went by, and Darwin's physical body was getting weaker day by day. Then he lost his eyesight. Therefore, starting in 2005, I began to take over his spiritual duties. During that time, he was helpless to make any physical arrangements because of the condition of his body and the people around him. History keeps repeating itself.

Now you can imagine my struggle and frustration during all these years. Paul Ji's lifespan was cut short, as he was poisoned, which led to his early death. And due to that, many circumstances changed. I still have some good friends within the organisation. One remarked, "It seems like you were one of the candidates after Darwin in 1981." I said to him, "I was the only candidate. I don't know where the others came from." He used the word *candidate* as if we were fighting some political election.

About myself—after leaving Barnhill Secondary School in 1971, I went to Southall Technical College and gained qualifications as electronics engineer in 1976. I did not practise in the field, but later I preferred to become a gas engineer. At present, I am a gas engineer, and it helps me to earn my living. I do not believe in living on Seekers' donations. These donations should be used to spread the message of God—nothing else. The rest is all history.

Since 20 March 2008, some people are still finding it difficult to believe in me. That is fine. Someone said that I was one of them, sitting in their satsang, and asked, "How come now he is the Master?" Darwin could become the Master after following the teachings for less than three years. For God's sake, I had been following for the last thirty-two years! Those remarks clearly indicated jealousy.

During my high times as well as my struggles, I have been sitting in disguise alongside you, never letting you know who I am. Despite that, if I had told you, I know that you would have never believed me; I had no proof, apart from a few glimpses that Spirit has shown you regarding myself. Out of those glimpses, I remember these remarks made by my satsang members:

1. "I think you are a Vairaagy Master." This Seeker was helped on many occasions.
2. "Yesterday, you appeared in my third eye during meditation. You were giving me discourse in a different language, which I understood at that time, but now I forgot."
3. "I was stuck in the higher planes. Upon mentioning your name, the lord of that plane let me go through." Spirit had shown clearly to this sincere Seeker that I was well known soul in these planes.
4. "I was standing in the garden 'Daytime'. I was stuck with some building work and thought of you to help me. You appeared physically out of the brick wall and helped. Thanks!" Yes, I still remember this appearance, and you'll be surprised to learn that now he has disappeared. Well, I am still very happy for him.

The list is endless. What I learned over the years is that it does not matter how much you do for people; they all have a very short memory. They forget very soon and are ready to walk over you. This is exactly what people had done with Darwin. We must try to learn the truth before making a final decision. A sincere request made to Spirit is never denied. But if you want the answers to be to your liking, they are not given. You cannot dictate to Spirit what to do. This is what Masters do.

We make a sincere request and leave it in the hands of Spirit, and Spirit listens. During this discourse, I hope that you have learned "the signs of a born Master". Before they were just words to mention—what Paul Ji had said long ago. Paul Ji has given the approximate age of the person at that time (see *E..........: Illuminated Way Letters*, January 1971, page 230, second paragraph). "He is now in training but where he is, nobody knows and won't know for a long time yet".

The final line on page 232 reads, "Only one who has not come out of his childhood yet." This was an answer to some, who were asking him whether they were the ones. It was a clear statement from Paul Ji regarding the age of the next Master:

1. He is not our member at the present time and will not be for a little while yet. Paul Ji's forecast was 100 per cent correct. That's why I joined in 1976.
2. I was still under twenty years of age that time. As I had worked with Paul Ji spiritually, he loved to execute his statements with full details. Reading a few books and following someone for a few years does not turn you into a Master. I don't think I have learned much in this life that I did not knew before, apart from a little touch here and there to suit the present time.

As far as I am concerned, I am just another soul among others.

I have plenty of patience. "From Spirit, you just can't hide." This is what I was told once, and the same applies to everyone. Well, I am still around.

BHAKTI-MARG (MEDITATION)

First of all, we are fortunate to follow a spiritual path such as this. As Paul Ji mentioned, we are the chosen ones. This term, the "chosen one" is very uplifting, and it makes you feel special. It simply means that you have created or gained enough good karma to be in such a position. Your good karma is responsible for this yearning within to seek further, so you can be in the presence of your creator. Once you have managed to find a present spiritual Master, you set up a goal—what you want to achieve in this life.

It is my job to remind you what that goal is and guide those who are willing to listen and follow. I do not wish to see people who are making sand-castles that have no foundation. When a little tide comes out of the sea, everything vanishes without a trace. This is a very common practise among followers of all religions. The followers want to achieve spiritual freedom from this world, but nothing materialises because no one tells these followers what to do and how to do it.

Every person is satisfied by material gains. All of the spiritual leaders are deeply involved in material gains too. So how can they ask their followers to do something different? To be a saint is not an easy job. Only one person out of a million will be successful. So, if you want to be the one in a million, the task is not easy. I am glad to say that some of you are working hard nowadays. When we read the history of past gurus and their achievements, we feel motivated to do something worthwhile.

They have worked very hard to make their mark in this world. Contrary to what Paul and Darwin said, to do a half hour meditation on a daily basis is not the same thing. I have been analysing the results from the last forty years, and I do not see any positive results from this. I have not seen anyone doing half an hour meditation daily and becoming a saint. I don't think Paul and Darwin were happy with the results either. The followers have become too relaxed.

The more lenient the Master becomes, the lazier the Seekers are. It was said earlier that Seekers should do a half hour of meditation daily. During that time, if the Master wanted to give any experience, he would. If not, you stop. We followed that over the years. This phrasing "if the Master wanted to give any experience" indicates very clearly that the onus is placed on the Master and not the Seeker. If you are satisfied with this gesture of spiritual experience, that is fine.

This lenience of the Master will never lead you to become Master of your own universe. So, when are you going to be the Master of your own universe? It was the achievements of earlier saints, such as Mahatma Buddha, Muhammad, Sai Baba, and many more—it was this spark within—that led you to set a goal for yourself. Now I will give you some examples of how they came to achieve what we know today.

Guru Nanak

Guru Nanak hardly did any hardcore meditation, as he was in contact with God all the time. He managed to spread the Word of God by word of mouth, as well as in writing so people could benefit in the future. He was naturally born with all of the abilities that a saint required. A spiritual light appeared at the time of his birth, and the shadow of tree protected him all day. He was a born soul traveller and was able to take anyone with him.

There are hundreds of examples of Guru Nanak's miracles in writings available today. We all praise his miracles, but we all fail to ask, *what did he do in his past lives to achieve this?* We all want to achieve what he achieved, but we don't want to do anything to materialise it. I hope this statement of mine brings a turning point in your life.

Jesus Christ

Jesus Christ is another great soul. There is not a single person in the whole world who has not heard his name at least once. This is such a great achievement for any soul. Again, he was not an ordinary person. That was due to his hardcore meditation during his past lives; it was this meditation that led to his fruitful spiritual life. Many saints forecasted his birth or the arrival of the Messiah. We all know the famous story of his birth and the miracles he performed during a very short span of time.

I am sure you want to do the same. But what are you doing to materialise your goal? God gives a chance to each soul to make its mark in this world. Some take advantage of this, while others leave this world unknown. You will be given another opportunity, but when? That is not for you to decide. But at this moment, you are sitting right in the centre of this opportunity. I would not miss this opportunity for anything in this world.

Mahatma Buddha

Mahatma Buddha was born with very good karma. That was why he was born as a prince and heir to the throne, but he was not born with any enlightenment. So, this is someone with whom you can compare yourself as a struggler. Once he came to know the truth, he began his search, which was not easy. He tried most of the meditation techniques and eating less food till he was almost all bone, but nothing materialised. He gave up on all the systems that had failed him, but he never gave up his hope.

He knew that the truth was somewhere and that he had yet to find it. He gave an ultimatum to himself and to God. He sat under the Bodhi tree and made up his mind that he would not get up from that sitting, even if he were to lose his physical body. After forty-nine days, he received enlightenment. So, making up your mind is the crucial point. We fail to stand by our goal.

Muhammad

Muhammad was the second person after Jesus to become a household name. Although God sent him as his prophet, he used to meditate within a cave known as Mount Hira on a regular basis. He was a very wise man, and at the same time, he had spiritual knowledge. This is another example that answers a common question: How important is meditation? You need spiritual experience. Otherwise, you will have no legs to stand on, to claim this status. Once you know who you are, you don't have to prove this to anyone.

Sai Baba

Born in 1838, Sai Baba began meditating at a very young age. During his youth, people began to believe that he was a miracle man. He faced lots of rivalry in his day, but truth always prevails. Nowadays, he is very popular within the Asian community. He was a spiritual dream man and soul traveller, and there are many evidences of his supernatural powers. He made his mark in this world, and I do not wish anyone to leave this world without making a mark. At the end of your lifespan, you should be able to say, "This is my spiritual achievement."

Baba Harnam Singh

Of "Bhuchon Kalan" was here in the eighteenth and nineteenth centuries. He also began his meditation at a very young age. During his youth, his first sitting was for one year. Then he got up for a little while and began his second sitting in meditation that lasted continuously for two years. His third sitting was also for two years. You may be wondering how he managed to sit for all that time. Once you make up your mind, the physical body is maintained with spiritual food from spirit.

You may laugh at what I am going to say next, but I have noticed something that happens during our half-hour spiritual chant. Once the words, "May the blessings be," are mentioned, most of the followers begin to stretch their bodies, as if they have just finished a hard labour—working a twenty-four-hour shift somewhere. You have to be serious about what you are doing. The goal you have set earlier is not easy. All I can say to you is that, you do have the capability of executing it.

Baba Harnam Singh, once he was recognised as a saint, began to meditate in a dark room "basement" but set no time limits. Once, he invited one of his disciples into the room, "Bhora", to ask if it was day or night outside. Out of curiosity, the disciple asked, "Why do you ask this? He replied, "Within this room, the sun is always shining, so I could not judge what it is outside." If you were in a similar situation, would you be afraid of a dark room? I doubt it very much.

Baba Harnam Singh's most famous disciple is known as Baba Nand Singh. Born 8 November 1870, he also began his meditation at a very early age. After moving from place to place, he finally came to stay in the small temple of Baba Harnam Singh. After spending twelve years of hardcore meditation under his supervision, Baba Nand Singh received enlightenment. Baba Harnam Singh then asked him to go to Nanak Sar and do his own preaching.

This indicates very clearly that, once the disciple becomes master of his own universe, the guru does not hold you any further. This is where the term *assistants* come in. Despite receiving all this power, he meditated all day and every night. I know the exact spot where he used to sit for meditation. You will be surprised to learn what kind of spot that was. It was open farmland, and there were many wild animals. No animal would dare touch you while you lean within Spirit.

Half of our members are afraid of little spiders. I am just giving you a reminder of how much stronger you need to be. He had all the abilities I can think of—light and sound, soul travel, spiritual and psychic scanning. Above all, he could turn his body into a lion, if someone did not listen to his instructions. Baba Nand Singh and Baba Harnam Singh both were very temperamental people but only if it benefited the disciple. Our members have a very vague picture of the character of a true guru.

They think that he is all smiling and goody-goody. That is not true. A good comparison is when we use our ability to discipline a child. If we do not discipline the child, he or she will grow up ignorant and tyrannical, used to getting his or her own way. Baba Nand Singh's very famous disciple was Baba Isher Singh, born 26 March 1913. After lots of meditation, he received enlightenment in 1950. He preached Sikhism at the same place till 6 October 1963.

The reason for mentioning this line of master-ship is that Spirit will never fail any person who makes a sincere effort in meditation under the instruction of his or her guru. This is why I am trying to provide all the ins and outs of spiritual tools. You never know which of these tools will lead you to a spiritual awakening. I was fortunate enough to meet and stay in the presence of Baba Isher Singh a number of times.

After receiving enlightenment, Baba Isher Singh made a special basement room "Bhora" and on the ceiling he fixed a U-shaped metal bar. Every night, he would tie his hair to this hook and meditate, while standing all night. Now you may wonder why he meditated this much after he'd received enlightenment. He did this because, once you become responsible for large numbers of followers, loads of karma drops on you like a ton of bricks.

To clear all that, you have to build spiritual stamina to manage the karma load. As Baba Nand Singh forecasted my birth, so I have grown up listening to their way of life. I contemplating on what I should do to achieve similar enlightenment. I did follow in their footsteps. And as you can see, it reflects in my character. This is the school of hardcore meditation. I do not wish to see anyone failing. You don't have to become a hardcore mediator, but do the best you can. Your effort will be fruitful.

If you are not willing to spend any time or effort, then that also is your choice. There is nothing you can hide from within. I may be temperamental at times, but it is only for your benefit. If someone thinks that this is not on, then I will say, "You have not joined the spiritual school yet."

WHIRLPOOL

Whirlpool is an amazing theory of nature. It can take **within** whatever comes in its way, and nothing will come out easily—unless sheer effort is applied and someone is there to guide you. Otherwise, you will never be heard of, who you are or were. I have created this freehand sketch to give you an example; whatever comes in its circle is sucked in. In the lower worlds, this whirlpool is known as Kal, and it has five very sharp and illusive fangs.

These five fangs spare no one. Similarly, there is a natural black hole in the sea. If a boat or a ship is travelling nearby, the vessel is pulled with natural force into its circle and taken down to the bottom of sea, never to come out. Some scientists were doing a practical experiment, and they purposely pushed a little boat in the direction of a "black hole"; it took the boat in, and the boat disappeared forever.

(Whirlpool Picture)

A Tsunami came a few years back out of the sea. This time, big floods came out of the Indian mountains recently, and they destroyed whatever was in their way, including Hindu temples. Many thousands of people were dragged away with this powerful flow of water and have not been found since. The Asian media has declared it "the tsunami out of the mountains". It does not matter how good we are scientifically nature always reminds us who is in control.

So, we have to learn the way of nature, and "soul travel" is the natural way of leaving these lower worlds. Soul travel can be done or performed in many ways. I am sure you can find your own interpretations of this theory. Within the last few discourses, I have been giving different theories to work on. I am sure something will help you to get out of this very wisely created "whirlpool" for the souls. The five passions are part of this whirlpool.

All I can tell you is that, if there is a way in, there is always a way out as well. I am sure you will find it. All of the religions are part of this great game of whirlpool. The word *chakrayvuh* (labyrinth) was used during the Mahabharata War, the times of Sri Krishna. It was a special technique to enter into the circle of enemy soldiers and then, in reverse, to get out of this circle to win. Only the living teacher can teach you how to enter the chakrayvuh and how to get out.

This is very easily done by entering into any religion. But do the varying religions have the teacher who can guide the followers in terms of how to get out of the whirlpool and find freedom. You people are sitting right at the bottom of this whirlpool being very happy that you have achieved your goal, when you have not even managed to scratch the surface of it. You had the living Master and the spiritual and book knowledge required, but you never bothered or managed to give it a practical shape.

As we all know, this is our training ground for soul. The word *karma* is the way to lead you into this whirlpool, and the living Master is the way out. This whirlpool of lower worlds has been created purposely by our creator to train souls. There are so many systems in this world better known as religions. All the religions are known or believed to be spiritual by their followers, when they are nothing other than a system run by some trained people in religious verses.

These priests are more stuck than normal people because they have become part of the roots of the whirlpool by their deeds. It's about time to make use of our spiritual knowledge and put it into practical shape. Slowly but surely, move out of this whirlpool and have a breath of fresh air on the surface of the ocean. Now, we'll look at some of the famous religions of this world to see where they will lead their followers.

As Jesus once said, "There are two sides to a coin, head and tails; one belongs to this physical level, and the other is spiritual. Now, the link to this spiritual side of the knowledge is lost to the majority of religions. They try to express everything on a physical basis, yet believing it is spiritual. This leads nowhere other than to the bottom of this whirlpool. Speaking of his kingdom, Jesus said, "Follow me." Later, he stated, "There are many mansions in my father's house, and I will prepare the places for you."

He was talking about the higher spiritual planes. He was never interested in anything on a physical basis. He said, "My kingdom is not of this world." Nowadays, his followers are knocking door to door and talking about creating the kingdom of heaven on earth. Now, can you see that the whole message of this great man has been totally lost within two thousand years, with misinterpretation in the opposite direction?

You see, Jesus was trying to take his followers out of this whirlpool, when, now, his followers are leading the masses into the whirlpool. This is what happens when you don't have a living Master or teacher to put you on the right track. Sikhism is another example, as Sikhs don't believe in having a living Master after ten gurus and have accepted their holy book as the eleventh guru. There are some teachers. They are labelled as "derra-babas".

They are living Masters but are not recognised as the Masters of Sikhism. Some of these teachers are good, while others are pseudo-masters and are deceiving people. As they have found, this is the easy way of making money. The question is, why do people walk into their systems? There are some spiritual Seekers who are looking for a way out of this world. Their respective religions failed to provide any answers. All religions lead the person to physical disciplines.

Now who will lead the individual to the spiritual side or show him or her what to do next? Sikhism is a great religion. The philosophy is based on the journey of soul into the lower worlds, and the final destination of soul is in the soul plane. There is too much politics involved in this religion, which is a setback for the followers. If someone manages to have spiritual understanding, he or she begins to look somewhere else to find the answers to his or her questions.

This is a true fact. Today there are more people leaving this religion than new ones joining. The Sikhs fail to spread the true message in many ways. It is also a fact that large numbers of people are joining Christianity and Islam on a daily basis. Islam has its own limitations, because Muslims do not believe in reincarnation system. So, the question of how to get out of this whirlpool does not even exist. Islam is talking about providing angels to serve the people who become the martyrs for this religion.

No true religion of this world agrees to any killings. So, the followers don't even know, what they are dying for. Now you can see, all these millions and billions of people are led to this whirlpool. First, there are not many who can show you the way out. Secondly, people themselves do not want to get out. They are so deeply involved in the five passions of the mind—lust, anger, greed, attachment, and vanity. Science today is leading the way, because all of the religions fail to provide the proper answers.

Politics has to be removed from the religions if they are to have any success. I will not be surprised when, one day, people will ask, "What is religion?" We fail to spread the true message of God so people can find their way into reality. In our teachings, the majority of members failed because they found the easy way—that is, to request that the Master solve their problems or physical ailments.

Now you realise that your problems have never ended, and your physical ailments are the same or worse. The Master has solved lots of your problems and taken the burden of your sufferings. We all witnessed this in Darwin's body. He went about sorting out your problems and pains so you could get out of this whirlpool. But you adopted the relaxed mood.

Now you know that your problems will never cease as long as you are living in the lower worlds. Nor will your physical ailments. So now it's about time to decide what you want to achieve in this life. I have no problem taking on your burdens. But then I know you will never be as strong as I want to see all of you become. I want to see everyone better or stronger than I am. I am sure you will not let me down.

ALIENS

Aliens have fascinated the human mind for a long time. Some are curious to know what they look like. Others may be scared because there are some stories about aliens based on the abduction of humans. A few claimed that aliens have placed some kind of electronic devices into their bodies. At the same time, some doctors claim to have removed these devices. Some people claim they are in contact with aliens on a regular basis.

Only these people can tell if they are telling the truth or if their claims are just a publicity stunt. Many of these people's stories are found to be hoaxes or frauds. Aliens communicate via telepathy, and they can travel through physical objects because of their vibratory rate. The questions are, can aliens overpower humans? Does any government have evidence of aliens? The sightings of aliens are reportable to the police and in turn the information is always passed over to the ministry of defence.

Because this agency is responsible for our security. Our imagination about the aliens is always wrong, because we try to scale all things on our physical parameters, while their vibratory rate is different. Their presence could be out of our reach to see them, unless they prefer to show their presence to a group of us or to a chosen individual. We only came to know about the aliens a few years ago. Some people must have had some kind of encounter with them and described what they saw.

In those days, cameras were not available like they are nowadays. Some people claimed that they had been abducted and some unknown experiments were carried out on them. They do not acknowledge what took place because their memories have been wiped out. After hearing their stories, scientists have used hypnotism to revive the experience so as to know what these people had seen. Others also claimed that some kind of genetic experiments were carried out on them.

So that, in future, a half-alien race could easily mingle among us. It is known as a future-breeding programme. This could be our future, as humans are going to create very dangerous ailments by over-using chemical experiments, which will lead to the destruction of the human body. So, they are going to prepare something to face the problem. Humans have very limited future foresight into what could take place.

The people on the astral plane have the full list of what is going to take place as time goes by. All our future inventions are already on the astral plane, and the ideas will be released to our future scientists through the dream state or semi-conscious state. The information can be released into our subconscious state, from where we can pick up these ideas at any time. The way we represent the look of aliens is totally imaginary. They are shown as semi-developed people.

In pictures, they appear to have abnormal looks, skinny and with long limbs. This proves that no one has seen them. They come from higher regions with very high vibrations and technology. Don't you think that they should look better in appearance than us? We know that they are our paranormal visitors and they travel from one galaxy to another. They are our visitors from the lower part of the astral plane and they use spacecraft we call UFOs (unidentified flying objects).

They use the planets, including Mars or Venus, as their way stations and visit this physical plane for many reasons. As the astral plane is responsible for the well-being of earth. There are very few chances that their travelling vehicles can become or get faulty. We hear many stories about a UFO crashing at a certain place and that the army captured the survivors. When we, or any scholars, try to investigate the evidence, it turns out to be a hoax.

The astral plane is out of reach to many, but current science is aware of our solar system, so people use the imagination to relate them to one of the known planets. Are we able to see them? Where have they come from and why? Our knowledge is very limited. Even if aliens do land on earth purposely or due to failure of a UFO, we must analyse the whole story with a sceptical mind to know whether it is true or false. Our judgement should be based on the evidence produced.

The planet Mars is well known for the possibility of an alien civilisation, since we have landed our spaceship on Mars. So far, there is no evidence of seeing or meeting with aliens or human life on this planet. We must have core evidence before making any claims. All the claims made back in the 1940s and 1950s were found to be false or hoaxes. We know most of our solar system due to the scientific progress within the last few decades.

The British Ministry of Defence has a UFO desk and a number of secret x-files. I wonder what their findings are. Back in 2002, a British man, Mr Gary McKinnon, hacked into secret American files because he was fascinated by UFOs and aliens. It was in the news that his secret hacking was caught by US authorities, who asked for his extradition. After ten years of legal battle, he was let off. In the early days, aliens were described as looking very similar to ET, extra-terrestrials with a big bald heads and slim bodies.

The descriptions developed into depictions of semi-humans, with some expressing an appearance very similar to lizards. Lately it has been accepted that their looks are very similar to humans or better. Some believe that aliens are intervening in our politics and giving guidance to some well-known politicians, suggesting what to do. This is a possibility. If we look back in history, we see that most of the inventions that have you made our modern life, what it is today, came to our famous inventors from somewhere else.

Either the aliens gave them the ideas, or they dreamed and landed in the museum in the department of future inventions on the astral plane. It is possible that aliens do come to earth because our control or powerhouse is on the astral plane. Similarly, the control for the astral plane is on the causal plane. The responsible authorities on the astral plane are concerned about our well-being. They make sure that the balance of everything is maintained.

Some believe or say that aliens are going to land on earth to control or dominate us. There are many imaginary theories regarding some kind of invasion, and many believe they will enter into our physical bodies and dictate their message through us. Many believe that, at one point, we will all be half human and half alien. Many people don't realise that these aliens are already living in a better place, as all the higher regions are better than earth.

Do not forget that the physical plane is on the bottom or lower scale of living. Do you think that aliens will leave a better standard of living and join us to suffer? You can draw your own conclusions. Many people do not realise that we are offshoots of these people, not vice versa. Aliens pay us visits; that is possible. Aliens are recognised by our scientists while "Jama-dutes" (angels of death) are recognised by spiritual studies. At the end of the day, Jama-dutes are also aliens to this world.

They are also of two kinds "dutes", representatives of Spirit, and Jama-dutes are angels of death sent by the king of the dead. Jama-dutes are well known throughout this world. Any person can witness them while on his or her death-bed due to old age or some kind of serious sickness. A person has to be semi-conscious to this world and on the verge of entering into the next world. In this state, many people are able to talk to their loved ones, who are sitting near-by.

This is what they are witnessing. Very few people who have this experience get better. But a few become healthy through good luck and tell us what they have seen and where they were on the higher planes. Jama-dutes always appear at the perfect time, when someone is going to die. And they also know who is going to die, so there is no mistake. This shows that they are aware of our every move and whereabouts. This is a clear indication that the astral plane has full control over us.

So, to witness some UFOs or aliens is a minor thing. They have the ability to pass through our physical objects because of their high technology or vibrations in spiritual terminology. They come quite often to do various kinds of experiments, but we fail to see them because they are out of our physical range of knowingness. The theory of devils, demons, or witches of the East or West is different. These are the souls of accidental deaths.

Due to the accidental nature of their passing, they fail to go back to the astral plane, so they cannot come back for another incarnation. We have lots of black magicians, and some manage to abduct these souls and control them for some misuse. So, this is another phenomenon. In the early days when minds were simple, when someone witnessed a UFO, it was considered as a visit of Gods. Compared to our physical senses, it is all a supernatural phenomenon.

The appearance of these Spirit objects is evidence of their existence. The UFO phenomenon is real. We can accept this or not. But the British, US, and many other governments have the evidence in their secret files. There is no limit on the shapes of these space objects. They could be round discs, triangular, or square, and their sightings have been reported since the eighteenth century. You may remember in November 2006 a UFO was spotted hovering over Chicago's O'Hare Airport.

Another one was seen later in March 2007 in Cleveland, Ohio, where we held our worldwide seminar in October 2008. We should be able to visit these higher regions, provided our present scientists can go beyond the speed of light and sound. We have to break this barrier of speed. Once this is done, most of our present well-known religions will fade into the background. They have failed to provide what they claim on a spiritual basis. People believe in evidence, not in mythological stories.

The way our science is progressing, it is not that far into the future when a visit to the moon will be available to everyone. The astral and other planes will be next on this list. This theory will be based on Spirit because the advancement of science will merge into spiritual theory. It will be a very common conversation among people: "When did you last visit the astral plane?" The theory of The Way to God will survive because we have to answer to our future science. The truth comes out slowly but surely.

There is no truth in the theory that earth is hollow or flat, with many layers underneath it. "Gnomes" living under earth is another false phenomenon; our scientists have already disapproved this theory with modern technology. A Greek mathematician named Mr Eratosthenes, who was born in 276 BC, proved that this world is round and the circumference of the globe is about 25,000 miles. It was Sir Christopher Columbus who sailed the full circle of this world in 1492 and discovered it is round.

So, there are no Patalas (subterranean layers within or under this globe) as believed by some religions. If you look at the sun, the moon, and all the stars in our galaxy, they all appear to be round. What then makes you think, that the earth is flat? First, we are influenced by our religious mythology. Second, there is a lack of education. A sceptical mind is always asking for evidence. So far, most of the religions have failed to answer people's questions.

The majority of photographs and video shoots have turned out to be hoaxes. The day will come when the evidence will be available. As the saying goes, "There is no proof without evidence." This is why I have said time and again that most of our present religions will fade away, especially those who are claiming to be the only ones. A question is often raised as to why aliens are shown with two eyes, one nose, and one mouth, very similar to humans.

Why don't these aliens have four eyes and four ears? This is a good argument. But from my experience, it does not matter which plane you are on; we all have similar features. The only difference is the vibrations we carry. The rate of vibrations will indicate our authority over others. This is why aliens have more authority over humans. Many farmers have claimed that aliens came and made circles in their crops; these claims all turned out to be hoaxes.

Such circles can be made very easily without a single foot on the soil as evidence. Some sceptical minds often ask, If the aliens are visiting us on a regular basis, why don't they make contact with us openly? It is not that they are keeping everything secret from us. We fail to see them because our vibratory rate is not the same or comparable to theirs; this is the only reason. In other words, we are a less spiritually advanced civilisation. It will not take long for the humans to turn into the alien race.

At present, we are moving very quickly in that direction. If we look back at our human history, we were fighting with fists and then with sticks and then with swords and spears. And then we took up pistols and then multiple shotguns. At present, we are already involved in nuclear wars. And what could be next? "An alien War? And that will lead us into the end of Kali-Yuga. Asian religions have always believed in aliens. Recently, Christians also believe.

A statement was issued from the Vatican on this subject. I wonder if the Pope has witnessed any aliens or UFOs. There is also a blue book in the Ministry of Defence that records the sightings of UFOs, and in it, over 10,000 sightings are recorded. There are two very famous people, Mr George and Mr Billy, who have lots of snapshots in their possession. How genuine are these photographs? Only they know the truth.

Mr George Adamski (from the United States) claimed that he was taken by the aliens to visit the solar system and that he and the aliens were on the planet Venus. But he could not prove this.

PHYSICAL UNIVERSE

In this discourse, we will discuss what is within this physical universe, such as planets and galaxy of stars, and how they affect our lives.

The solar system

The solar system is the combination of nine planets, asteroids, comets, moons, and a galaxy of stars. They all are placed with the command of Spirit; with their distance from each other, their heights, and their push or pull, they are all in balance. There is a micro millionth of difference in push or pull to each other and the sun. This difference makes them to orbit the sun, and at the same time, they rotate on axes at some degrees. The nearest planet will orbit in less time.

For example, Mercury is 36 million miles from the sun, and it orbits the sun in 88 earth days. Pluto, on the other hand is the farthest from the sun, 3,665 million miles away, and it orbits the sun in 248 earth years. This is why our present scientists have found that each planet rotates at different speeds. This rotation keeps the whole environment healthy below the astral plane and right down to this earth planet.

Secondly, their celestial brightness amuses our minds, and this amusement leads us to search and attempt exploration of these planets. This amusement has been created purposely by the Spirit, for the purpose of learning for all the souls. In the early days, 20 July 1969, man went to the moon. Since then, farther journeys have been made to different planets. At present, this travelling is via spacecraft called rockets.

Eventually these space-craft will improve as the travelling goes deeper and deeper or higher and higher. This search and improvement of our spacecraft, as mentioned in the chapter on aliens will help our science go beyond the speed of light and sound of the physical level. Eventually, these space-craft will land in the astral plane. Then migration of our physical or human bodies will be to the other planes. This travelling will be via astral bodies.

In future, we will learn how to leave our physical bodies to the side, similar to leaving behind our garments when we change our clothes. We as humans always like to migrate to better countries or places where we find some excitement. This is why a poor man wants to migrate to a country where he can prosper financially. Those who have seen enough financially or have enjoyed a better standard of living probably like to study the animal kingdom or sea life.

It always has been believed that aliens from other planets are going to invade earth. I wonder sometimes, what excitement will they find here? This probably will be the most boring place for them, unless they prefer to waste their time here. Once we enter into the astral plane, only then will actual exploration for the soul begin. This exploration will be available at our fingertips. The experience is for the soul, and the excitement is for the mind; and it will lead the "soul" near and close to God.

During the golden-age, our third eye was visible to communicate within God worlds on a spiritual basis. In the future, this communication will be spiritual and scientifically based. This urge to find what is new and the poor conditions of living on earth, due to our maximum chemical use and the reactions of those chemicals, will force us to migrate elsewhere. At present, the population of this planet is on the rise or in a growth pattern. But due to the circumstances mentioned, this trend will be on the decrease.

The fertility of all species and earth will be at almost halt. This world will be like a ghost town. We will create this condition ourselves, just as this happened long ago on Mars and Venus. This is why our scientists are suspecting life on those two planets. Yes, there once was life. In future, this statement will apply to us too. With more exploration, we will find this evidence. Human population will be a lot smaller. At the same time, our scientific improvement will lead the humans remaining to leave this planet.

It will be about time to close the chapter of Kali-Yuga. The remaining souls who could not manage to earn enough good karma will be put into deep sleep in physical terms or a spiritual bliss state. They will remain so until a "new" physical world is ready to begin—the new chapter of Satya, Treta, Dwapara, and Kali-Yuga. Those souls who were in bliss state at the end of the last Kali-Yuga will wake up, and new physical bodies will be given.

They will be the first on the next Satya-Yuga, but their karmas were not good enough last time to allow them to leave the physical forever. Their siblings will be of a new creation, as there is long chain of inexperienced souls in waiting. Similar to the last time, in the beginning, these humans will have holy thoughts. Eventually, their thoughts will be contaminated with negativity, and that will lead them into Treta-Yuga. The whole cycle of Yugas will repeat.

What is solar system? Solar system is everything that centres or circles around the sun. The difference between the universe, galaxies, and solar system is size.

Universe

Universe is the largest of these three because all three are included within the realm of this universe. Scientists believe that this universe is expanding all the time. Yes, this is the law of nature. Did you ever contemplate the thought that everything in this universe grows and moves? This includes humans, animals, and plants. Otherwise, they are declared as no more. There are a number of planets that are in between what already has been discovered, and the border of astral plane is yet to be discovered.

Galaxy

Galaxy is the total of what we can see in the sky. As mentioned earlier, all that we see there is held together within this big void or empty space by the push-and-pull system, currently known as gravity. This galaxy is the total of billions of stars and planets, and they are always on constant move. This universe is moving all the time via means of Spirit or light and sound. Scientists believe that it is some kind of gravity upholding the distance between each planet or the stars.

We call it Spirit because everything was created by it. We may notice that some of the stars are "in still position" or at the same place since we were young. This is because our present lifespan is too short in comparison to this minor movement, so we do not notice any change. Our present science does not commit when it comes to the movement of these stars, but they are moving and expanding; this is the law of nature. This movement is not that significant and can be put in to some calculation.

This movement from A to Z, known as 360 degrees round the sun, will take millions of years. At present, our lifespan does not exceed much over 100 years. So, to take any notice of any change in the position of these stars is impossible. We can notice the change in some celestial bodies, such as earth, the moon, Mercury, Venus, and Mars. The solar system is the smallest of three systems in question, as it consists of the sun, moons, asteroids, comets, and meteoroids.

Astronomy

The discovery of planets and stars within our galaxy and their positions in relation to each other was a result of the dedication or contribution of Indian Hindu philosophy, as well as Chinese, Greek, and Babylonian societies. In a real sense, all the planets are stars too because they shine. Astronomers are the people who are very dedicated to the study of galaxy. They examine the movement of these planets and make note of any new discovery. Astronomy is a vast subject; different departments deal with different subjects, such as:

1. Cycles of stars
2. Structure and interaction of stars
3. Entire universe structure

Astronomy is a natural science, which is the study of celestial objects such as stars, galaxy, planets, moons, and nebulae. It involves the study of physics, chemistry, and evolution of such objects—whatever is within this universe. To make this possible a telescope was required. The telescope was invented by someone else around 1600 CE, but it became famous in 1609 CE when Galileo Galilee presented it to this world. He discovered the rings around planet Saturn.

He was born on 15 February 1564 in Pisa, Italy. He was a physicist, mathematician, and engineer. Now you see, on the physical level, you need certain types of skills to educate the mind and leave this treasure for the generations to come. Galileo left very valuable information from his study and observations, which helped present science to progress further. Darwin and I made visit to all the planets, moons, and the galaxy of all stars.

This experience was noted in my diary dated 27 September 1979, which will appear in our new book. I was taking this visit as a personal study in those days, so I did not bother to make any notes or write what I witnessed. Now Spirit has asked me to write on this subject to explain what I saw, so I'll try to cover it as briefly as possible. At present, my fellow Seekers are struggling to achieve their goals—despite being so close to me physically and spiritually.

And guidance is given so openly at present. For example, many years ago, a telephone was very rare and the use of phones was very limited. At present, you can find the whole world in your mobile phone, and that is in everyone's pocket. In the same way, this present science will turn into spiritual science, and all this travelling and spiritual knowledge will become a way of life. First, they will go against all the religions because they fail to provide any evidence but eventually the way to God will appear and show them the way.

Then, the change in this universe will be instant, and the gates into heaven will open. Take the discovery of our known planets and the findings of our scientists, such as their names, sizes, and the distance from the sun. The sun is the centre point, around which all the planets circle, and there are number of moons on each planet. This distance is measured in miles, and earth is 93 million miles from the sun. This is a known factor.

It has been considered by our scientists to call the distance 1 AU (astronomical unit). All other planets are measured according to this one unit, and science has already discovered almost 150 big or small moons. The big moons are in this chart. The sun has the strongest gravity of all. That is why all planets orbit the sun.

Name of Planet	Size of Planet miles Diameter	Distance from the Sun Million miles	Moons	Orbit time
Sun	865133	0000	0	0000
Mercury	3032	36	0	88 Days
Venus	7520	67	0	225 Days
Earth	7901	93	1	365 Days
Mars	4201	140	2	2 Yrs
Jupiter	83100	482	17	12 Yrs
Saturn	67576	885	18	29 Yrs
Uranos	31041	1780	21	84 Yrs
Neptune	30256	2790	8	164 Yrs
Pluto	1429	3665	1	248 Yrs

(Nine planets chart)

EARTH PLANETS

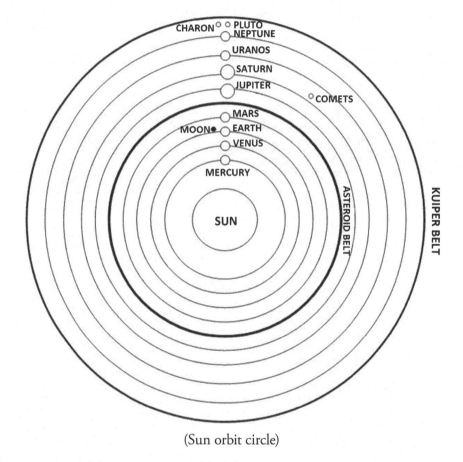

(Sun orbit circle)

Mercury, Venus, earth, and Mars are inner planets. Planets between the asteroid belt and the Kuiper belt are outer planets, as they contain more gas on the surface than the inner planets. The word *planet* is the translation from one of the Greek words that means "wonderer". It means all the planets orbit the sun while all the stars are almost in fixed positions.

Sun

The sun is the biggest planet of all. It is also the hottest and the centre of all the planets. And due to its strongest magnetic field, all known or unknown planets orbit sun. Its surface area is 11,900 times that of earth, and the diameter is 865,130 miles. It is composed of 75% hydrogen and 25% helium, and the overall colour is yellow. The surface temperature is 5,600 degrees Celsius. The light coming from the sun reaches earth in eight minutes and twenty seconds.

It travels at the speed of 186,450 miles per second. The sun is 93 million miles from earth. It is believed by our scientists that sun has already used or burned half of its hydrogen. The closest planet to sun will orbit faster than the farthest ones, due to the difference in circumference and magnetic field. The temperature inside the sun is approximately 15 million degrees Celsius. As you notice, it has a very high temperature. So, it can explode any time. But due to its enormous gravity force, everything is intact. The sun is responsible for the earth's climate and weather changes.

Sun is the cause for rainbow to appear. The light from the sun as it appears to us is white, but in effect, it is the total of seven colours. You will notice we only see rainbow during certain weather conditions. This is why the word *rainbow* is taken from rain. Those hanging drops of rain in the sky act as a prism, and once this white light passes through the prism, it splits the colours into seven. They are always in same order—red, orange, yellow, green, blue, indigo, and violet. Why we see sky as blue and red at sunset is due to similar theories.

Mercury

Mercury is the first or closest planet to sun. This is why its orbit period is 88 earth days. Mercury appears in our earth sky in the morning or evening but isn't visible at night-time. That is because of its orbit condition in relation to the sun. It is much fastest than any other planet. Its atmosphere is very cold. The temperature is in the range of –180 degrees Celsius at night-time and up to 430 degrees Celsius during the daytime.

The polar diameter is 3,032 miles. One day on Mercury lasts up to 176 earth days, and the distance from the sun is in the range of 36 million miles. The gravity is approximately 38% comparative to earth. Being the closest planet to sun, Mercury does not experience much of the seasons as we do. The temperature is very cold compared to that on earth, even though it's so close to sun.

This is what we call nature. So far, two spacecraft have visited around or near this planet. *Mariner 10* went in 1970, and *Messenger* was launched in 2004 and is still there. The surface of Mercury is mainly "rock", and it is the combination of 70% metallic and 30% silicate material. The planet's density and gravity are very similar to those of earth. Metallic content is higher on Mercury than any other planet.

Although the surface is very similar to the moon, no man has set foot on this planet because our scientists believe the environment is very toxic. It has acidic rains and very high-speed stormy winds, and the surface is uneven rock. The surface and atmosphere are the combination of hydrogen, helium, oxygen, sodium, calcium, potassium, and icy surface. The magnetic field is very strong, due to its surface properties.

Venus

Venus is the second planet from the sun. It was named after the Roman goddess of love and beauty. It was discovered in the seventeenth century, and its orbit period is 225 earth days. The surface temperature is 460 degrees Celsius, and the diameter is about 7,520 miles. A day on Venus is longer than an earth year. It takes 243 Earth days to rotate once on its axis. The size of this planet is smaller than earth, and it is 67 million miles from the sun.

Satellite on or at Venus is none. Venus is the second brightest star in the sky, so it can be seen during the daytime, provided you know where to look at. The atmospheric pressure is ninety times greater than that on earth. It is very similar to the bottom of sea, so humans could not survive. They would be crushed or exploded into small pieces. Similar to on Mercury, there are no seasonal variations.

Russia was the first to send spacecraft to Venus, in 1961, but failed. Their second attempt, with a Venera series probe was launched in 1966. At one point, it was believed that Venus had a tropical atmosphere, so life on this planet was possible. Now it has been found that the planet has a very dense atmosphere due to high temperatures. Its humidity is very similar to a greenhouse, and it's known as a hostile environment. The overall surface has very dense clouds of sulphuric acids.

Earth

Earth is the third planet from the sun. Its diameter is approximately 7,901 miles, and it orbits the sun in 365.26 days. This is why we have 366 days every leap year. At the same time, it spins a full circle in 24 hours. When we are facing the sun, it is day, and when we are opposite, it will be night-time. Earth's surface temperature is 14 to 57 degrees Celsius. Earth's inner and outer core temperature is 6,000 degrees Celsius. In size, it is much larger in comparison to moon.

In the early days, it was believed that earth was the centre of this universe and all the planets were orbiting or circling earth. At present, we know that sun is the centre of all the planets. Earth is approximately 93 million miles from the sun. Earth's name comes from the Anglo-Saxon word *Erda*, which means "supporting life soil". This is the only planet that is habitable to human life and vegetation. Its habitability is due to the 21% oxygen in the air of one volume, that it has water as liquid on the surface, and that it has a layer of soil to retain heat.

The latter is responsible for vegetation growth. Its natural satellite is the moon. Earth is not as round as we believe. It has a slight bulge towards the equator. That's why it rotates on its axis at 23 degrees. This axis at 23 degrees and the planet's 365-day orbit of the sun are responsible for all four seasons. Earth has 3% fresh water, which is pumped out of the soil or in the form of ice. The rest is salt water or other fresh water, which evaporates into the atmosphere and returns as rain.

Moon

The moon is in synchronous rotation with earth. That means the same side will always face earth. The moon orbits the sun once a year or in 365 days, the same as earth because earth and moon orbit the sun at the same time. The moon orbits around earth in 27.32 days, and its polar diameter is approximately 2,159 miles. Surface temperature at night is –170 degrees Celsius, and it's 125 degrees Celsius during the day.

Russia was the first to send spacecraft to the moon in 1959. These were a robotic mission of crafts called *Luna 1* and *Luna 2*. On 20 July 1969, the Apollo 11 mission was launched by the United States of America, and Mr Neil Armstrong was the first man to set foot on the moon. Missions Apollo and Luna returned home with at least 380 kilograms of rock and soil for future testing.

Effects of the moon

Our monthly calendar is based on the moon's effects. The moon is our natural satellite and provides us light at night. It was very useful when electric illumination had not yet been invented. The effects of moon have been linked to crime, mental illness, disaster, and birth and fertility. But werewolves and Dracula are mythical characters created by our writers or filmmakers, much like Superman and Spiderman. A number of psychic people engage in occult rituals, and they claim to receive black energy.

In Hinduism, **Karva-Chauth** is a one-day festival celebrated by Hindu married women. They fast from sunrise to moonrise for the safety and longevity of their husbands. They will only open the fast once they see the moon.

In Islam, **Eid** is also connected with the moon. It is mentioned in the Qur'an to sight the fresh moon to begin the month of fasting and end the fasting on sighting the end of the moon cycle.

Solar eclipse

A solar eclipse is when the moon passes in front of the sun and casts a shadow on the earth. Although the sun's distance from earth is around 400 times the moon's distance and the sun's diameter is 400 times greater than that of the moon, as seen from earth, moon and sun appear to be the same size. That is why moon covers the whole face of the sun at that particular time.

Sometimes, it is not full eclipse, as the moon and earth are on different points because of their rotation, so the moon only manages to cover half or part of the sun. There are two to five small eclipses every year. The longest solar eclipse is every eighteen months, and it lasts approximately seven minutes and thirty seconds.

Mars

Mars is the fourth planet from the sun, and its surface colour is sunset, so it is known as the red planet. Its atmosphere is primarily composed of carbon dioxide. The planet's polar diameter is 4,200 miles, it is 140 million miles from the sun, and it has two moons. Mars doesn't have any protective layer of soil, so it cannot store any heat. That is why it is much colder than earth.

Mars average surface temperature is –55 degrees Celsius and 20 degrees Celsius during midday. It is less than half the size of earth. Gravity on Mars is 33% in comparison to that on earth. Mars orbits the sun once every 2 years, and one year is equal to 320 earth days. Seasons are very similar to those on earth but longer. It is believed that "lava" is always active.

Although forty missions to Mars have been made, again Russia was the first to launch. *Marsnik 1* went in 1960. Later, other countries followed. This planet has the largest dust storms. These storms can last for months, covering the entire planet and rendering visibility of anything dim. It is very rich in iron, similarly to other planets. So far, no known life has been found on Mars.

Jupiter

Jupiter is the fifth planet from the sun, and it is 320 times larger than earth. If all the planets were combined together, Jupiter would be 250% bigger in size. It is next in size to the sun. Jupiter is made up of gases so it is known as a gas giant. This is one reason that it doesn't support any life. Its polar diameter is 83,100 miles, and its surface temperature is approximately –108 degrees Celsius.

It is the fourth brightest planet in our solar system. Only the sun, the moon, and Venus are brighter. Jupiter is one of the five planets that are visible to our naked eye from earth. It is named after a Roman god. The day on Jupiter lasts only approximately ten earth hours. It orbits the sun once every 12 earth years, so weather patterns on the planet are the second reason Jupiter's conditions aren't very healthy to support life.

Jupiter is 482 million miles from the sun. The planet's interior is composed of metal, rock, and hydrogen. Jupiter has seventeen moons, Ganymede being the biggest moon in our solar system. And above it has a ring system composed of icy dust particles. So far eight spacecraft have visited Jupiter. An automated spacecraft launched for Jupiter in December 1973.

The major problem on Jupiter is that it has no solid surface on which spacecraft can land. The atmosphere on this planet is made up of liquid and there are very high radiation levels. Because of these conditions, many systems on spacecraft attempting to explore Jupiter failed on many occasions.

Saturn

The sixth planet from the sun, Saturn, is 90% large in size comparable to earth, and it is the third largest planet in our solar system. Saturn was discovered by astronomer Mr Galileo Galilee of Italy, who invented the telescope in 1609 CE. the planet polar diameter is 67,570 miles, and it is

885 million miles from the sun. It has eighteen moons and many small moons and surface temperature is –178 degrees Celsius.

It is the fifth brightest planet in our solar system and can be seen by the naked eye. Saturn is one of the flattest planets (discs), whereas other planets are oval or round in shape. It has very low density and fast rotation. It turns on its axis every ten hours thirty minutes approximately and has the second shortest day in our solar system. It orbits the sun once every 29 earth years. It is mainly composed of hydrogen, and the atmosphere is composed of ice, water, rock, methane, and frozen nitrogen.

The first spacecraft to reach Saturn was *Pioneer* back in 1979. It has a very strong magnetic field in comparison to that of earth. Saturn has rings around it made up of "ice grains", and they look fabulous. The planet's composition is 96% hydrogen and 3% helium; the remaining 1% is made up of ethane, methane, water, ice, and others things. This composition of gases shows no sign of any life on this planet. Gravity is very similar to that on earth.

Uranus

Uranus is the seventh planet from the sun and another gas giant. It is not possible to see with the naked eye. A telescope is required. It is a rolling round planet, with its spin axis lying 98 degrees off its orbital plan with the sun, and its polar diameter is approximately 31,000 miles. It was discovered on 13 March 1781 by Mr William Herschel.

Uranus turns on its axis, once every 17 hours and 15 minutes, and its orbit is in the opposite direction of the orbits of the other planets. It orbits the sun once every 84 years, and it is 1,780 million miles away from the sun. Uranus is composed of hydrogen, helium, rock, methane, and frozen ammonia water/ice, so it reflects blue and green colours. It being another gas giant planet indicates there is no possibility of any life.

The upper surface is made up of water, methane, and ice crystals, which makes it the coldest planet of our solar system. The surface temperature on Uranus is –220 degrees Celsius. Uranus has two sets of rings, about thirteen rings in total. It has twenty-one moons and a number of small moons. So far only one spacecraft has passed by this planet. That was *Voyager 2* back in 1986.

Neptune

The eighth planet from the sun, Neptune is the most distant one and another gas giant that is not visible to the naked eye. Its polar diameter is 30,250 miles, and surface temperature is –210 degrees Celsius. It was discovered on 23 September 1846. It spins round in 19 hours, and it orbits the sun once every 164 earth years. It is 2,790 million miles away from the sun.

It is one of the smallest ice giants and again it is composed of hydrogen, helium, methane, water, ice, and rock. Overall, the colour of Neptune is blue with thin clouds and very high-speed winds. Neptune being another gas giant, there is no chance of human life, and similar to Jupiter it has a number of rings. It has eight moons and a number of small moons. It is one of the coldest planets.

So far, only one spacecraft has passed by it—*Voyager 2* in 1989.

Pluto

Pluto is the ninth planet from the sun, though lately it's not considered a planet but only a dwarf planet. It is the smallest of all planets in our solar system. Though not recognised as a proper planet, it has its own moon named Charon. Surface temperature is –220 degrees Celsius. Pluto makes one journey around the sun every 248 earth years, and it is 3,665 million miles away from the sun. It was discovered back on 18 February 1930.

Pluto is composed of dangerous gases, such as carbon monoxide, methane, and nitrogen. It orbits the sun on a different plane than the other eight planets, going over or below in circle. Pluto is only 1,429 miles wide, and its moon Charon is 745 miles wide. **One day** on Pluto is equal to approximately 7 earth days, and Pluto is only visible with the help of telescope. Density on Pluto is very light; 100 kilograms on earth will act like 7 kilograms on Pluto.

On 14 July 2015, United states first spacecraft flew above the surface of Pluto.

Charon

Charon is one of the fifth moons relating to Pluto, and it was discovered in 1978 by the United States. Since, four more moons have been discovered, bringing Pluto's moons to five. Charon's temperature is approximately –220 degrees Celsius, and its orbital inclination is at 96 degree and rotation period is 6.5 earth days. Much like earth's moon, Charon also keeps the same face towards Pluto during its rotation. Charon is covered by frozen water, and as the moon, it does not rise or set but remains the same all through.

Kuiper belt

The Kuiper belt is made up of billions of ice objects. It is like a frozen edge or boundary over all the planets—composed of ice, methane, ammonia, and water. It could be the crossing line between the physical and the astral planes.

NASA

The National Aeronautics and Space Administration is the US agency responsible for the nation's space programmes and similar research. Most of US space exploration is the effort of NASA, who put the first man on the moon. The agency is also responsible for space stations and space shuttles and international space stations. NASA was formed back in 29 July 1958, and its headquarters are in Washington DC. It is the contribution of NASA that gives us practical insight on these planets

Satellite

A satellite is an artificial object intentionally placed into "orbit" with the help of rockets. Satellites are computer-controlled systems. They are used for many purposes, such as for military services and civilian earth observations. In this world, there are approximately 6,500 satellites. At present, approximately 1,000 are working actively, and the rest are out of date or known as debris. The first satellite was launched on 4 October 1957 by the Soviet Union.

Russia was the first to make a move into space. But at present the nation is not doing well, which has been the case since the break-up of the Iron Curtain. The United States always followed in Russia's footsteps, launching its first Satellite on 2 January 1958, and rest of the world is third in line. Nowadays there are a number of space stations that have been launched. Again, it was Russia who launched Salyut 1, the first space station of any kind, on 19 April 1971.

ASTROLOGY

All these stars and planets are for a purpose, and they are affecting every single person who is living in this universe. How they orbit around the sun and the way they rotate will create an effect. Each star sign in our present astrology represents one or more planet in the house. As I said earlier, all these planets are moving. Any person's present or future is dictated by the position of these planets at the time of his or her birth. This is why having a correct date of birth is very important.

Fortune tellers are fully trained in this field to know what to look at. Nowadays, some people have worked quite hard in this field; they have managed to feed all the information into computer systems. Based on date and time of birth, including the minute, as well as place of birth, any person who has the desire to know the future will be given the information within seconds. The future is based on your karma, your date of birth, and the position of these planets at that particular time.

Experts in astrology use a number of charts, normally with twelve sections (houses), and work out the position of these planets at the time of a person's birth. Or they may determine in which house a particular star sign was at the time and what other planets were affecting it. Then there is time limit for these planets to move from their positions. Some move faster than the others. It is the movement of these planets that brings changes in our good or bad luck.

This movement of planets also affects the chemistry of our physical bodies. Many species depend on this movement or the position of moon. The population of this world is totally dependent on earth, moon, and sun. There was another experience dated 8 April 1980, when I was taught about Para vidya. Para vidya was released to me, and the significance of the numbers 3, 5, 7, and 12 was revealed.

The solar system is a vast subject. It does not matter how much you have written it is never enough. There are very dedicated people who have spent all their lives on this subject. This search can be traced back 15,000 years. What is written so far is totally basic knowledge or information. Different researchers have their own opinions. Many times, more than one planet is ruling your star sign.

ZODIAC SIGN	DATES	SYMBOL	PLANETS	ELEMENT	SEASONS	HOW MANY MOONS
ARIES	21MAR--19APR	RAM	MARS	FIRE	SPRING	2
TAURUS	20APR--20MAY	BULL	VENUS	EARTH	SPRING	0
GEMINI	21MAY--21JUN	TWINS	MERCURY	AIR	SPRING	0
CANCER	22JUN--22JUL	CRAB	MOON	WATER	SUMMER	Itself
LEO	23JUL--22AUG	LION	SUN	FIRE	SUMMER	0
VIRGO	23AUG--22SEP	MAIDEN	MERCURY	EARTH	SUMMER	0
LIBRA	23SEP--23OCT	SCALE	VENUS	AIR	AUTUMN	0
SCORPIO	24OCT--21NOV	SCORPION	MARS	WATER	AUTUMN	2
SAGITARIUS	22NOV--21DEC	ARCHER	JUPITER	FIRE	AUTUMN	4
CAPRICORN	22DEC--19JAN	GOAT	SATURN	EARTH	WINTER	9
AQUARIUS	20JAN--18FEB	WATERMAN	SATURN	AIR	WINTER	9
PISCES	19FEB--20MAR	FISHES	JUPITER	WATER	WINTER	4
			EARTH			1
			URANUS			6
			NEPTUNE			2
			PLUTO			1

(Twelve star signs chart)

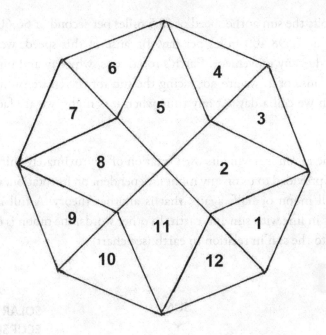

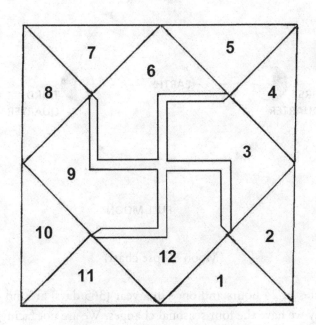

(Two-by-twelve section charts)

Earth orbits the sun at the speed of 18.5 miles per second or 66,600 miles per hour or 1,598,400 miles per day. Because of this speed, we do not acknowledge any movement. Earth's rotation is, why day and night take place; because of it, we are not facing the sun for the entire twenty-four-hour span we call a day. At any time when it is night, we are facing the moon.

Again, the moon is having its own rotation of approximately thirty days. The light provided to us on any night is dependent on its rotation, whether it is a full moon or half; again, that is another theory. A full moon is when it is in line with sun and earth. In other words, the moon is equal or opposite to the sun in relation to earth (see chart).

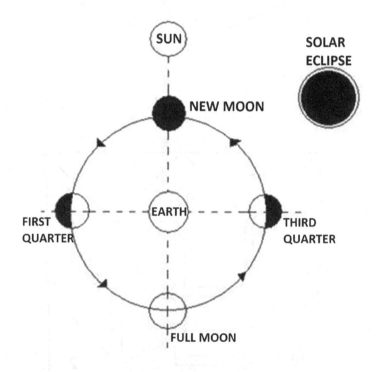

(Moon eclipse chart)

Earth rotates in 24 hours and once in a year (365 days) around the sun. That is why we have the four seasonal changes. We are not facing the sun fully all through the year. This rotation of earth is also at 23 degrees, so this is another rotation within the main rotation. Leap year is part of this—365.26 days or 366 days. In other words, earth's rotating at 23 degree itself, and at the same time it is rotating round the sun. This is responsible for long days and short nights or vice versa.

Within the last few years, our scientists have managed to bring back samples from some of the planets. This will help us to learn, and it will encourage future exploration. This exploration will go further and further. As you notice, all the planets are circulating around the sun. Where the circles of this universe end, next are the circles of the astral plane, and then further inner circles will be explored with new-found technology. Now the question is, who was the first person to study these planets and stars?

What were his capabilities for doing this? And how effective were his calculations? Although our knowledge about the planets and stars that nowadays we call astrology comes from the contribution of many countries and regions including India, China, and the Islamic world. There was one person who lived beyond our recorded history whose calculations are still used today. They are being challenged by many scholars, who have been unable to find them wrong. His name was Rishy Bhrigu. We will discuss his findings in next chapter.

China

Astrology in China can be traced back to 3000 BC. Chinese astrology is very close to its religious philosophy. Key components are three harmonies, which are heaven, earth, and water, and the principle of yin and yang. Yin means negative, and yang means positive. It is their belief that, if both are maintained in balance, harmony is accomplished. It is very similar to the karma theory of keeping everything in balance in order to have a good and happy life.

Babylonians, Iraq

Babylonian contributions can be traced back to 2000 BC in the form of thirty-two tablets with inscribed liver models.

World-wide

Worldwide, astrological studies can be traced back to 3000 BC. It was the dedication of advanced thinkers in their respective countries who came to know that some of these "stars" were moving that led to our current knowledge. Later, it was discovered that these celestial bodies were also affecting us on earth. Still later, we discovered that the big stars are actually "planets", and this led to further exploration.

At present we know enough. But our knowledge is not even a scratch on the surface. All these stars or planets also move, and this movement is known as breathing. In this universe, everything has to move and expand. Otherwise, it cannot survive. This is the law of nature.

RISHY BHRIGU

Rishy Bhrigu was a saint of Brahmin caste, and his residence (ashram) was on the bank of the Vadhusar River, presently on the borders of Haryana and Rajasthan, India. During the times of Lord Vishnu, he was the son of Sage Varun. He was chosen by other saints to test Brahma, Vishnu, and Shiva to know who was the greatest Master. When he went to see Lord Brahma, he disrespected him; Bhrigu cursed Brahma, telling him that he would not be worshipped in Kali-Yuga.

He paid his second visit to Shiva, where Shiva and Parvati were sporting fun so entry was not granted. He cursed Shiva, saying that he would only be worshipped in linga form. His last visit was to Lord Vishnu, who was in deep sleep. As Lord Vishnu did not respond to his visit, Bhrigu felt insulted. He got angry, and on his way out, he hit Vishnu in his chest with his foot. Upon awakening, Vishnu asked for his well-being. Then Bhrigu declared that Vishnu was the greatest.

Laxmi witnessed the whole incident and got angry and cursed him—that you Brahmins will never see the face of Laxmi (money) and all your caste people will face poverty. Bhrigu explained the purpose of his visit, asked forgiveness for his negative act from Laxmi, and requested that she free him from her curse. Laxmi calmed down and pardoned him. However, she said, "I cannot free you from this curse. But I ask you to write an astrology book that will help your caste people to earn their livelihood."

Being a saint, Bhrigu was capable of writing this book, and it was given the name of *Bhrigu Samhita*. Originally it was written on palm leaves in Sanskrit language. Later it was translated to Tamil. Bhrigu managed to write 525,975 different calculations to cover each minute of the year, including leap year (365.26 days). It is believed that *Bhrigu Samhita* can only be used after performing some rituals. Then a page from the book will open itself as required.

Rishy Bhrigu was the most original person to study the planets and stars and their effect on humans. His original book was only one handwritten copy on palm leaves, which was the property of the Brahmin caste. India has been invaded by many races, so that book has gone underground. The books we see today claiming to be this writing are copies of that book. But many are inaccurate, while others are frauds.

These 525,975 calculations can be turned into a calculation for every second (525,975 × 60 = 31,558,500). These many calculations were required to cover every single date of birth, in relation to time and the position of the planets. The horoscopes were drawn according to the position of all planets, such as the sun, Mercury, Venus, earth, the moon, Mars, Jupiter, Saturn, Uranus, and Pluto. Rahu and Ketu are two nodes.

These are "still-time" readings but flexi readings over millennium could be as many as 28.4 million. All other countries came later to provide astrological readings. *Bhrigu Samhita* displays the art of preparing the chart, known as Janma-Kundli, which is equivalent to Zodiac signs. Saint Bhrigu's predictions are comparable to the Akashic records, so they can tell the past, present, and what will happen to an individual in the future.

Most of the information fed into our present computer system is based on the calculations of Saint Bhrigu. It is believed that some copies from the original writings are kept in Banaras, Puna and Meerut. Things were made easy for the Brahmin caste for the generations to come. They can look into the past, present, and future of anyone who is interested to know at some charge.

It is believed that Saint Bhrigu lived some 10,000 years ago in India. One thing always astonishes me—Hinduism is relating saints such as Bhrigu and others with Brahma, Vishnu, and Shiva. The time mentioned as

10,000 years is totally out of date, given these three lords have not set foot on this earth on a physical basis for hundreds of thousand years.

Hinduism

Hinduism claims that Saint Bhrigu was here in Treta-Yuga, and that is also the beginning of Hinduism. I don't want to know at what point in time of Treta-Yuga he was here. After Treta, Dwapara-Yuga came, and it lasted approximately 864,000 years. Now Kali-Yuga has extended over 5,120 years. I notice Hinduism is underestimating itself in many ways; Hinduism knows what the truth is but has no evidence.

THE EFFECT OF PLANETS

Sun—Surya: The sun is the king of all planets, so it is considered as life-giver to all. The effect of the sun creates one's unique identity and creative ability, how one faces challenges in life, and strong willpower. So, it is the most powerful planet. Medicine effects are heart, circulatory system, bones, and eyes.

Mercury—Buddha: Mercury is the messenger planet. It brings good luck. The effect of Mercury is achieving good results overall. It is the planet of mental communication. It is concerned with super-intelligence. Mercury people are always communicative and strong personalities. As for medicine effects, Mercury is associated with one's nervous system.

Venus—Shukra: As the planet of beauty and love, anything pleasant is the symbol of Venus. Venus is the driving force behind one's behaviour. Venus is a sociable planet. It has the capability of building relationship and is responsible for emotional satisfaction. So, it represents the circle of Spirit and love. When positive, a Venus person is charming, affectionate, and artistic. In medicine effects, Venus relates to veins, throat, and kidneys.

Moon—Chandra: This planet is known as the soul. It represents the child within us. It is known as a creative and receptive planet. The positive effects are a well-settled nature and harmony at home. The moon is of feminine nature and has great concern for self-security and for others. Medicine effects are the digestive system, breasts, menstruation, and the pancreas.

Mars—Mangal: Mars is the planet of strong willpower and "ego". Its effect on us is that we are courageous, energetic, bold, strong individuals. A Mars person will have aggressive urges and may lose his or her temper if things are not done. At the same time, Mars is associated with unluckiness of brides. Medicine effects relate to the masculine system.

Jupiter—Brihaspati: Jupiter is the planet of justice. A Jupiter person will have the qualities of moderation and kindness and greater insight into religion and philosophy. Jupiter people have the ability to explore the self and always want to go further in life. They are willing to take risk. In medicine, this planet is associated with the liver, the pituitary gland, and disposition of fats.

Saturn—Shani: As the way shower of God or duty, Saturn relates to the ability to control one's self, including self-discipline, persistence. A Saturn person is a hard task-master. Such people don't prefer to waste time, are good time keepers, feel happy in mental maturity, and may experience loneliness.

Uranus—Indra: The planet of the awakener, Uranus is related to overall drive for freedom and independence. Uranus people are not much interested in whether or not they are socially accepted, as they feel ahead of the surrounding atmosphere. Always willing to challenge injustice, they are true individuals or very unique people. Medicine effects include the nervous system, mental disorder, hysteria, spasms, and cramps.

Neptune—Varun: Neptune is the God of the sea and drive to transcend and the planet of vision. Neptune people are aliens to others in thought because of their individual character. Their visions are beyond normal thinking. Medicine effects include the spinal canal, neuroses, and the thalamus.

Pluto—Yam: Pluto is the planet of wealth. Pluto people will have the drive to transform themselves, as Pluto is the planet of renewal. These people are quite tuned and not to be taken very lightly. Medicine effects include regenerative forces in the body, involving cell formation and reproductive system.

Charon: A Charon person will have the drive to heal his or her self-image and the willpower to overcome any sufferings.

Two nodes—Rahu and Ketu: Are Chhaya (shadowy) planets. They are the life paths, known as dragon. These are two points of north and south, opposite each other, where the moon's path crosses the ecliptic. North represents the dragon's head, and south represents the tail.

SCIENTIFIC FACTS OF HUMAN LIFE

Similar to others, Christians are the same regarding the birth of Adam and Eve. According to their scholars, Adam and Eve were born approximately 6,019 years ago, when our scientists are talking in millions of years. For example, scientists are finding human bones whose laboratory tests reveal their age to be far beyond these religious years. This is a clear indication that a real saint has not existed in these religions for a long time.

Their scholars have no authority over proper timings, as they cannot look back into the past to trace proper record of when the events took place or to look in to the future. To find out the truth, you have to have the knowledge of beyond time. Some believe that copies from the original *Bhrigu Samhita* on palm leaves are kept in Hoshiarpur library in Punjab. A Brahmin family is the caretaker of these writings.

These leaves are believed to be over 500 years old. Although saint Bhrigu was not from this area. Upon requests for readings, present pandits (scholars) in this library draw the charts after knowing your name, date, and place of birth. Two charts are drawn. Now they look for the identical copy of what they have drawn from or within these old leaves, as they are placed in bundles. The exact leaf is found.

It mentions the name and the purpose of your visit. Information is given about your past life, present, and some future forecast. Astrology has helped to drive the development of astronomy, and further studies lead us to explore these planets. Practical visits and the findings of our present science are contradictory to our religious beliefs. So, it is a learning point for us all. Sometimes what we see "is not", or sometimes what we don't see "it is".

1. The practical exploration of our scientists and their findings.
2. Astrology calculations, such as the movement of these planets and their effects on us.

NASA has declared there is no life on any planet, so there are no chances of any invasion. But to the contrary, we are trying to explore these planets, and that is invasion as well from our side. Now who are these aliens, who don't exist to us or us to them, if there are any? This is very brief information on the subject.

I could write three times more. I don't think that would be enough either. I hope you have enjoyed it. The list below contains some of the facts found by our scientists. They are not to be taken lightly by our religious bodies. Otherwise, one day you will know how out of step you have been. I can already see the results. Here are the facts:

1. The age of our solar system, according to the study and findings of our scientists, is 4.5 billion years.
2. The distance between all planets and sun is in the range of million miles.
3. Human remains found by Israeli archaeologists, date back to 400,000 years. A set of 8 teeth were found in a cave.
4. It is accepted that Homo sapiens were living in East Africa 200,000 years ago.
5. Human bones were found of at least 28 people in a cave in north Spain. DNA tests reveals they are approximately 400,000 years old. New York University confirmed with geological technique that these remains are older than 300,000 years.
6. 20 kilometres from Chandigarh, Punjab, India, French and Indian archaeologists discovered human remains. They're waiting for the final results, but they are saying these remains could be as old as 2 million years.

We cannot sit down and hold onto our guns and say we are always right. All I can say is that timing of the origin of Adam and Eve and of Hinduism is totally out of date. Other religions can be traced because they are not that old. These are only a few facts, but you can find thousands more.

POWER OF MEDITATION

The journey of soul and its spiritual success depends on how we do our meditation. This is the direct path, where you can experience spiritual journey live in this lifetime. To make it live, you must do your spiritual exercises on a daily basis and with full dedication. Your success depends on attitude and how you apply gentle attention. I am very disappointed with so many people I know, who have not even scratched the surface of spirituality.

Though they have been following the teachings for well over forty years. After all these years, the common complaints are the same: I cannot concentrate properly. My thoughts are wandering everywhere. I do not see the inner Master. I do not see the divine light or hear the sound. Recently many people have come to see me, and these are the common problems they are facing. For this, the reasons are many. I've come to the conclusion that almost everyone is not meditating properly.

First of all, do you know what you are following? Do you know the purpose of these teachings? Many are following because others or family are following. If you are in doubt, I should let you know these teachings are designed to train you to become a saint in your own right. Now the question is, are you prepared for it? If you are, make a fresh start. It is never too late. Every tool has been provided in my book *The Way to God*.

To access these tools, simply you read it thoroughly, once, twice, or more until you feel you have got to the bottom of it. If you do not understand, you can ask at the inner level or direct your questions to me. I am always so close. I love to help those who want to learn. Your success is my aim. I have noticed that cause for failure is that we are not meditating properly; very lazy methods are applied during this period. I asked one person, "How do you meditate?"

The question was raised when this person told me he was doing lots of Bhakti "meditation". What I noticed was, in real life, this person was suffering all known domestic and health problems. This person revealed that all the Bhakti was being done while lying in bed. What a lazy way of finding God. You are lying in bed and want to become or be under training as a saint. I've never heard of a single saint in history who was lying in bed and found God.

Saints are willing to follow any instructions or method regardless of how hard it may be to fulfil their desire to meet the creator. Sitting in lotus fashion is very common. During my travels in India, I have seen many saints stand on one leg for long hours and with minimum food. I do not wish for anyone to follow the path of asceticism, but our way is very simple. The recommended position is better known as tailor fashion.

If you do your meditation while lying in bed or on a sofa, you will face all the known physical problems. This is why I noticed that all our members are facing problems above average. I have come across only one or two individuals who said they are successful. The majority are in crying situations. This is another point. I never knew that saints cry. History is full of evidence, especially those saints who suffered at the hands of the villains.

Many were slaughtered, hanged, shot, or crucified. But till their last breath, they were reciting their spiritual word. They did not complain and took it as the will of God. The question is, what is or what was their strength? From where did they get this kind of stamina? The answer is very simple—meditation. They are in meditation all day and night. To them, nothing else bothers them or matters. With this recitation, you come to a point where spiritually you are so strong that no problem does or will bother you.

Problems do come into the lives of saints too, actually more than for an average person. All those people who are entangled in the problem world have a long way to go to achieve their goals. All these people who are crying, I wonder sometimes, what teachings do they follow? The same goes for those who do not leave their negative habits, which are too many to mention. To any person who wants to become spiritually strong and achieve some spiritual ground: "There are no shortcuts."

All these years, you have tried in relaxed methods and failed. To discipline yourself is the basic requirement. The meditation has to be done by sitting in tailor fashion or sitting on sofa chair with your feet touching the floor, your back erect, and your chin slightly up but in a relaxed manner. The recitation of the "word" during meditation has to be done un-interrupted for one hour. A half hour twice can be done in certain circumstances, but do not make a habit of it.

Apart from your meditation, you must recite your word during waking hours, till you sleep. The Spirit will take the responsibility of recitation during the sleeping period. I recommend you to read the chapter on fasting. It explains how you can manage to recite your word all day and every day. Your vibrations will be sky high and beyond; you will be **no-more** a crying baby. Now you will be the knower of truth and probably the way shower to the others, valued assistant to the Master, and of God.

Do you want to become the Master of your own destiny or be toyed with by your destiny? Those who are successful "rightfully," as the saying goes, experience a state where your feet are on the ground but you are dwelling in the higher worlds. We all dream of having this state of consciousness, but who wants to make this effort? Only a few. I think it's about time to wake up and be counted as one of Gods' own.

I will conclude this discourse with the words of a very famous poet, Dr Iqbal. But I have slightly changed them to give a spiritual message. This is how I recite this poem:

> Kabir tu kar tapp itna
> Ke har takdeer se pahle
> Khuda bande se khud pushe
> Ke bol tery rajaa kya hai

Here's a simple translation: Kabir, you do enough meditation--So before any destiny--God itself will ask you--What is your desire to be fulfilled?

With your meditation, you must achieve a very high state of consciousness. I was lucky enough to learn these four lines at a very young age. And I knew there are no shortcuts on the way to God.

WORD

Many people are not aware that the entire world and universes are run by the **word**. All the universes are created by this word, and we are having our being and breathing within this word. The word is the creative and communicative force of God. God breathes in and out to communicate with soul. In return, soul travels on the vehicle to communicate with God, which helps soul to become aware of its creator. With this awareness, soul becomes the knower "as I am it and it is me".

All the saints have emphasised the importance of the word. For Guru Nanak of Sikh-ism the "sound" is *anhad shabda*. In Christianity it is mentioned as *word*. Christ has been known as word made flesh. It is true, though many people are not aware, that Christ as a consciousness or soul was *word made flesh*. When any awakened soul takes physical body, that time it is word made flesh. As mentioned earlier, it is the creative force of God.

Many religions call it *divine light and sound*. Bani again is an indication of word, so *Elahi Bani* means God's word. Again, the word *Elahi* is driven from the word *Allah*. It is the name of God in Islam religion. The Elahi Bani means the word coming from deep within—that part known as the presence of God within each individual. The whole mechanism of the individual "soul" is based on this. Any awakened soul is searching for this word, so it can make its way to the creator God.

"Why do we search for this word? It is the craving within us. It does not matter who we are and what status we hold in this world. But there is something within us that is nudging and making us realise that there is something missing. With our good karma, known as spiritual unfoldment, we become the Seekers. Again, it is an individual search. I have seen some spiritual Seekers, when they are successful in finding the true Master, give the message to all their friends and families.

Many times, I have seen that all the family join or become members of the religious organisation run by this saint. Some people join because they become emotional after hearing some stories known as miracles. We cannot become Seekers on the basis of our emotions. This is why many people come and leave. We cannot expect all these people to be true Seekers. I do not know, what you understand about this one word, *Seeker*.

As far as I am concerned, the Seeker is a person who is on his or her way to becoming a saint. So, if you do want to become a saint, you'd better be serious. You cannot turn back or give up. You must strive towards God to achieve your spiritual goal. It is just like any athlete who learns to play any game at school level and later under the supervision of a coach, eventually making it up to the Olympics, must continually focus and strive.

Olympic athletes achieve a gold or silver medal according to their efforts. The guru or teacher is your coach. The guru will guide and teach; in return, you listen and practise.

The practise brings perfection. If you do not listen or practise what has been told, nothing is going to materialise. I have seen so many people who do not listen or practise properly and yet believe themselves to be serious God Seekers. For these people, nothing is going to materialise; it does not matter who they are following.

To a true Seeker, only few words of wisdom and small practise are good enough to make them live. They become live and this "word" is rolling within them day and night. The importance of the word can be explained in many ways. As a whole, there is a word known as the creative force, through which the whole world or all universes are created.

That particular word will not be suitable to all; it is as powerful as God itself. We will not be able to handle this power.

The guru is aware of our state of consciousness and will give the word during initiation, according to our spiritual stamina. There are millions and billions of words to suit the whole creation. Every spiritual Seeker must have his or her own word to suit vibrations. The word given by their guru is a special mantra. It is very similar to a placement of fuse in to the wire to make it live. Without this fuse, the circuit formed by the wires is known as open circuit; therefore, no current flows.

Any spiritual Seeker can read any known holy book in the world and as many times as possible; it will never make you spiritually live. It can give you an enormous amount of spiritual knowledge, but you will never become spiritually live. By chanting of your personal word, you can. You only need to recite it a few times during your spiritual exercise, as well as your waking state. Doing so helps to stir the vibrations at "third eye" to the level of sun and moon worlds at Ashta-dal-Kanwal.

That is the beginning point between the Seeker and Master to meet and where the spiritual journey begins. You can stay at the seashore by reading all the holy books and be loaded with religious knowledge. Or you can dive into the ocean with a single word. I have heard all of the religious leaders whose belief of a religion is on the basis of masses. They make fun of the concept of individuality. When they don't even have a clue, what we are discussing here.

Now what can you expect from these people? They are misled and instructing the same mis-guidance to their followers. The word given by your guru is secret and special; it must never be revealed or discussed with anybody. Once it is mentioned in the open, it will not hold the same vibratory rate or power as before. So, it may not work according to your spiritual expectations. The word is the activating ingredient in your spiritual life.

Keep it safe, as you need it every day until it will lead you to a point of spiritual advancement. Later your teacher or guru will intervene again to change the word, which can lead you to the next level of unfoldment. Your again, the guru is very similar to your sports coach, who can give you one exercise or one technique to lead you to Olympic gold medals. The exercises and techniques we practice have to be changed with our progress, whether it be sports or spiritual unfoldment.

There is always a plus element in all the fields. You must keep striving towards your goal until you have reached your destination or you are satisfied. Without the guru or the word, nothing is possible. But most religions are brain-washing their followers not to follow this kind of teaching. They are under the influence of fear—fear of losing you.

These people are not the well-wishers of your spiritual being. Any person can join me any time as they wish. At the same time, they can leave me any time as well.

To join or to leave is individuals' free will. I am here to teach individuality and will continue to do so as long as I live. That is all that matters to me and to the Spirit. God is individual, and it will remain the same forever. Thus, it is dealing with each soul on an individual basis. You are individual and yet part of God. So be counted as one of its own. Only your spiritual word can lead you to this knowingness, and one day you will become the knower of truth and teach the others too.

TREE OF WISDOM

Once upon a time, a seed was sown in soil. The person who planted the tree was a very wise man. He knew one day this seed would grow and become a tree of wisdom. A good thought was given before planting it, and all the preparations were made for the tree's future. After a few days, a small plant with two golden leaves appeared.

A new experience had begun. It already had a lot of wisdom, but there was still something to learn. The planter had tremendous love for this little plant. He watered the plant from time to time and talked to it. The little plant had good company and security, while its new assignment in this world took place. It was looking forward to the new experience.

After a short time, instead of two small leaves, a few small branches came up with a lot of leaves on them. It was a dramatic experience to go through the four seasons—spring, summer, autumn, and winter. It was learned that the leaves were not permanent; they would come and go. Winds came, snow fell, and many times the branches were pulled down by birds and children.

But this wisdom tree never complained. It had learned in a short time that to make a complaint was a waste of time. Complaints halt the progress. Every moment was a good experience; a new wisdom was received. It was a free gift to those who deserve it. Every year, the tree grew a little in height. During the spring it sprouted fresh leaves.

It was a good sight and pleasing to all eyes. But in autumn those leaves would fall. And that routine continued. The tree reached new heights, its branches were more flexible, its trunk was thick, and the roots were firmer. Now it was ready for any weather, any season. With ups and downs and the vagaries of bad weather, it learned the law of balance and of patience.

It understood "living in the present" and total reliance upon its planter. At this stage, the tree planter also knew that the tree was ready and he could, along with the others, enjoy the shade in summer and the sight and fragrance of the blossom in spring.

Now indeed it was a *wisdom tree*.

GHOSTS

We often use or hear these words: "What are ghosts?" A ghost is the Spirit of a dead person, especially one who is believed to appear in body form or likeness to loved ones or people in general or to haunt formers habitats. Sometimes they can appear in full flesh, and other times they come as shadowy visions. Some people are excited to tell ghostly stories, while others are interested to hear these stories. There are some who try to avoid because just listening causes a shiver of fear to run through their bodies.

Many will lose sleep because their dreams will be full of ghosts and they are afraid to sleep. They know as soon as their eyes are closed, a ghost will appear. There are some who will try not to go in dark room or space because they don't know what to expect. Now the question is, have you ever seen a ghost? There are some who don't believe in the existence of ghosts. There is good percentage of people who believe in or have seen a ghost at least once in their lives.

How does a person become ghost? There could be many answers to this question. There are many tell-tale stories with which I do not agree. It is a belief that a person who has attachments or greed and has lots of money but is not willing to share will not leave this world after death. We have seen movies made and books written on this subject, such as the well-known Christmas story featuring Mr Scrooge. These stories may not be true. But there are chances that they carry a sliver of truth.

If a person dies accidently or is killed under abnormal circumstances, then there is a possibility the Spirit of that person will not leave the physical arena or the place of living. Accidental death means the person who died was not expected to die yet, and the "angels of death" did not appear to collect this soul. Accidental death is a very startling experience for anyone. The spiritual journey soul was going through has been cut short, and now it has become a wandering soul.

This person, who we now call ghost, is going through a very disturbing experience. He or she can see us or loved ones but fails to communicate with us or them because the living cannot hear or see this person "ghost". There are chances that a person who has experienced an accidental death, sometimes does not even realise that he or she is dead. Not getting any response from loved ones could be a very frustrating experience to go through.

Some ghosts are helpless to harm anyone, as they are living in fear of further torture because of the circumstances by which they have died. Perhaps they have been through a very dramatic situation. They feel safe to stay within the boundary of their dwellings and try to hide in dark corners of the house. It is possible that, if you walk into that dark spot with a neutral state of consciousness, out of nowhere, you might see someone standing there.

A person with strong willpower may not get scared, while others could become mentally disturbed for many days. They will not enter that room in the future. Sometimes you cannot see but sense the presence of someone. These ghosts living in that room will always look after their belongings— the ones they had while living. If someone tries to touch or throw away things that belonged to them, they won't be happy and could get angry and try to teach a lesson to the person involved.

If you move something around for whatever reason in the room that person has occupied, when you come back next time, you'll be surprised to learn something you moved earlier is still in the same place it had been before you moved it—where it was sitting originally. Now that is a clear sign that someone's Spirit is there. Or you can give yourself the benefit of doubt and conclude that you did want to move the object but forgot to do so.

If you experience the same thing a number of times, then you know someone is there. It is advised not to interfere any more—that is, if you don't want anything unpleasant happen to you. There are many different kinds of ghosts—normal ghosts; accidental death ghosts or martyred ghosts; *cheel*, demons, devils, or negative energies; and hundreds more.

Normal ghosts; A normal ghost is one who passed away from the physical level and did not manage to leave this world. This kind of ghost is totally harmless. Accidental type ghosts are powerful, and at times, they can be very demanding from close family. They do hold spiritual or psychic powers to harm someone if the demand is not fulfilled. Their demands could be on regular basis and continue for the generations to follow, until a practitioner or a saint can show them the way to heaven or spiritual planes.

Martyrs; Martyrs are very powerful ghosts because they have chosen to die for a purpose. This purpose is most likely religious based. Those who die during the wars between two or more countries are also ghosts. They joined the army to serve their country, or they were forced to join, or some life circumstances pushed them in this direction. Joining your country's army, navy, or air force is a good thing, but no one can forecast what can be expected the next day.

It is not the soldiers who fight; most likely, you will find it is more or less political game. The soldiers who die will be buried or cremated with full honours, and medals will be given to the families. That is accepted practise in this world. But has anyone given a thought to the well-being of that soldier's soul? At present that soldier could be a wandering soul. Most of the soldier ghosts are helpful.

Once I was working as a gas engineer, and during my work, I became friendly with the person in charge of the premises. He was an ex-soldier, and I told him I would like to learn pistol or rifle shooting. He suggested that it is always best practise not to learn to shoot. Otherwise, once you know, it will lead to further exploitations. I agreed with his suggestion. He told me a very interesting real-life story about a fight that broke out in his country.

He was given the duty to guard his village, along with a few others, as he was an ex-soldier. He was not very keen to fight, but he could not refuse. It was night duty, but he loved his sleep. One night while on duty, he was in local cemetery and very badly wanted to sleep. While he was thinking about sleep, a ghost appeared, who was also an ex-soldier. The ghost told him to sleep next to his grave. "If someone comes," the ghost said, "I will wake you up."

At first, he feared this incident, but he chose to sleep.

After a few days, he felt comfortable with the ghost. This fight carried on for months. During that time, ghost would wake him up whenever he sensed someone coming. He said, "Once I'd gained my confidence that this ghost was helpful, I felt a lot better and enjoyed my sleep every night." He was very thankful to the wandering Spirit of this person who'd lost his life—under what circumstances, no one knows. Now you see this kind of ghost is helpful because they are trained in how to save lives.

Cheel; Is a name given to a female ghost who did not choose to die but was pushed to her death-bed by circumstances. This normally happens or used to happen when medical help was not available to the woman, who was giving birth to her first child, living in a remote area, or without someone available to help her at a time. When she was in pain. Child delivery at times could be easy with the first child; at times, it could be a nightmare, especially when there was no helping hand.

The child may have been born safely, or at times still-born babies were born as well. During this experience, the lady suffers the most dramatic experience. In a few cases, ladies used to die due to excessive blood loss. Now you can imagine the pain she has been through. So, she becomes "cheel". This kind of ghost is never happy because the circumstances of her death were not pleasant. She will never leave the place of her death.

If you happen to see a cheel, you will notice her clothes are covered in blood-stains. If you walk into that particular room and happen to see her, never challenge her by asking questions. She is also not very happy if she sees the new-born baby in the family. Her single touch to this child could result in the death of this child. This kind of ghost is powerful and can manage to give a full-blast punch. This is my very close personal experience.

Martyrs ghosts; Known as shahid, martyr ghosts are very powerful ghosts. They are the people who gave their lives to some spiritual cause or fight for righteousness. In Islam, this struggle is known as jihad. Christians, Sikhs, and Hindus have their own names. As the cause of their death is spiritual, this is their belief. And up to some extent, their thoughts were also spiritually based.

These ghosts or shahid can be very powerful, and they can be seen at times. Normally, they appear at places where some kind of religious war is taking place. Their visibility at times helps the soldiers to gain confidence or to boost the morale. I have heard numerous stories about these ex-saint soldiers.

Ghosts; There were a number of houses boarded up in Southall for years. I still remember two houses on Greenland Crescent and two on Lady Margaret Road and one in Park Avenue. They were on sale for years and very cheap as well, but there was no buyer. A number of people bought these houses, but ghosts would not let them settle peacefully. All who tried to live in them moved out, and all the doors and windows were boarded up.

I remember one story. A person was very excited to buy one of the houses on Lady Margaret road. He was so happy to decorate with clip art wallpapers. The next day, he went to admire his successful decoration. To his amusement, he noticed that all the flower prints were upside down. He gave up and boarded up the property. Nowadays, people are living in those houses, so someone must have managed to sort out these ghosts.

The Catholic Church does practise exorcism. So, what is it that they do? With their psychic knowledge or some spiritual recitation, the exorcist evicts the demon or Spirit ("ghost") from the body of the person or any building the ghost is inhabiting. Due to whatever circumstances, the ghost has entered the body of a person or taken possession of a dwelling. These practitioners ask the ghost to leave this person or place. You will find that Indian and Muslim newspapers advertise this practise as well.

In England, some time back, one hospital was in the headlines. A number of staff members saw the ghosts wandering in corridors and near the morgue area. At least ten complaints were made. Then the person in charge took action to sort out this situation. Experienced people were consulted, and things were back to normal. Later, it was discovered that part of the hospital building was built on a former cemetery. Now you see, many ghosts do possess their graves as well.

Groups of ghosts; Yes, if a ghost finds another ghost from the same area or comes across a previously known face, they will form groups and dwell where it suits the whole group to stay. I have seen a group of seventeen ghosts. They were all relatives, males and females together, and some others joined as well. How they came to this fate is a long story. Some were murdered, and others passed on from accidental deaths, and it all added up to this group.

Once I befriended the ghost, we were working on night shifts. Somehow, during our tea break, conversation on ghosts came up. It was just a normal conversation, but one person thought it was funny and began to joke on a daily basis. I said to myself, *'Enough is enough'. This person needs a lesson.* There was one dark room in our factory where people complained to the management a number of times of seeing someone in a white uniform, especially during the night shift. It was true.

There were actually five ghosts living there. They were people who'd worked there over a period of time. But the reasons they never left the place were not known. They used to appear at times but never facing you. As we were all printers, after finishing a particular job, the responsible person was supposed to hang his dirty printing dye in the racks of that room. Being the supervisor, I knew this joking person would be coming to this room soon. It was our night shift.

So, I made a request to these Spirit friends—it's about time to show your faces when he comes in this room. I stood in one corner to watch. He walked up the stairs and entered the room. While he was in the middle of the room, he saw the visions. He dropped the dirty printing dye there and then and ran downstairs to his working place. I made my way there before him to see his face. He was shocked, sweating, and speechless. It took him a long time before he could say, "I have seen the ghost."

I gave him a glass of water to drink and calmed him down. At the end of his shift, he went home and stayed in bed for three days with fear. When he came back to work, he told everyone what he had seen and advised the others not to joke about ghosts. Have you ever seen a live ghost? I see them every day. Surprised? During your travels while driving, you will notice lots of drivers don't move at traffic lights although it is green signal.

Their thoughts are far away. While walking, you bump into many people. They don't even know, where they are going. All these people are without any direction in life or suffering from depression. Many people would love to sleep twenty-four hours a day if possible. Those who do not recite the word of God are also without any true direction in life. In other words, they are wasting very valuable time. To all these people I call them "live" ghosts.

Are you one of them? Make the most of your time; it is far too short.

Guardian angels; Many people in this world have guardian angel. A guardian angel could be a former family member who is not living any more but protects you. All saints have guardian angels provided by the Spirit. That is why they walk anywhere and meditate in dark rooms without any fear. All those who follow a true saint, their living Master, will become the guardian angel for them.

Do you have a guardian angel?

SPIRIT

Spirit is the essence of God. Anything we can think or imagine or anything that materialises is all Spirit. God cannot show its presence everywhere, but via Spirit, it has established itself in totality. Any place ("temples"), writing, or speech with the mention of Spirit becomes spiritual. The whole of creation is based on Spirit. All of the solar system, the placement and continuous rotation of each planet, the distances between them— all this is controlled by Spirit.

This is why all religions mention that there is no place where God does not exist. The crux of the point is that the whole of eternity is assembled and sustained by Spirit. Spirit is divided into the two main pillars of God— divine light and sound. This is to enable our communication with God. With light and sound, we are always in the presence of God. Therefore, it is very important to open up to the light and sound to have any spiritual experience.

Although light and sound are always within us, to be aware of God consciously is most important. Otherwise, we are living in a day-dream state and not materialising anything fruitful. It is very similar to making sand-castles without any foundation, which will vanish with a small tide coming in from the sea. This is what I have been seeing most of the Seekers doing over the last forty years. The Seekers are depending on the experiences, which are given by the Master out of his love for them.

This is to raise their vibrations so they can make some positive effort. But they have become too reliant on the Master and have become passive. This passiveness is Kal's work, to keep the Seekers grounded in the physical. The day you join the teachings, you are live within Spirit, as the Master is the direct channel of God. Although Spirit is and has been within you all the time, you did not have the means to experience it live.

It has been recommended over the years that we should do at least one hour of meditation every day. That is good if you have a totally saint nature in living or practise. I have noticed over the years that, unknowingly, people are creating more karma on a daily basis that cannot be cleared within one hour of meditation. So, what is your gain on a spiritual basis? To eliminate our negative creation, we must live our life consciously.

The spiritual force is with us always to give a nudge whenever we are about to commit a mistake. However, this nudge is often ignored. Whenever you feel the nudge, do you know at that time that you are live within Spirit? This opportunity is not available to those on other religious paths. This is why they keep referring to their religious scriptures—when you can refer within. How much more practical do you want? When I say, "My love and Spirit always surround you", this covers all the religious scriptures put together.

All religious scriptures were within first. Later, the Masters managed to express this spiritual love in words. God establishes the Master on the physical level, so people will have more opportunity to know the truth. When you meet the Master and see the way he presents the discourse to you, you will know that he is the picture of "the truth". The Master wants you to know this; otherwise, his efforts are wasted. I am happy all the time, but I would be even happier if I knew that a number of Seekers had made success in their spiritual endeavours.

I put lots of effort in writing each month for your benefit so you can look at Spirit from another dimension. We must hold a 360-degree viewpoint. This is known as creativity.

Spirit is not limited in numbers. There are millions of experiences waiting for each person, but Spirit leaves this to the free will of individual.

Individuals can take this advantage or lead their lives passively. Many prefer to lead their lives passively, thinking there is plenty of time.

Well, forty years have already gone by without any solid consolidated experience. Time is very short, as I've mentioned in our book. In a few days, you might come to know that the "show is over". In the next life, will you have this opportunity to be in direct contact with the Master of the time? Only time will tell. I believe in the present moment. The opportunity should be taken *now*. I packed up my bags from physical work because Spirit is more important to me than anything else.

You can do the same if you have created the means to maintain your living expenses. Living on social benefits is not healthy. Spiritually, do you know the amount of karma you are creating or accepting on your account by doing this? Probably, your one-hour meditation only just covers it. So, what is your spiritual gain? Every single breath is counted, when you are living at the expense of others. Some people try to get away with it by saying it is within the law.

That is true, but when soul is facing the king of spiritual law on judgement day, what physical law you have been following will not be the king's concern. He is only concerned with what is in your spiritual account. Physical laws are man-made and do not operate in the spiritual worlds. I have given a very clear indication in our book that we must learn to give as much as possible, instead of being on the receiving end. Those who are genuinely disabled are excused for the time being, as they are helpless.

However, Spirit will find ways of providing a means of living for those disabled individuals, who try to use their creativity. Spiritual exercises are very important. Lately, I have noticed that some of you are trying very hard. That is good for you and for me as well. The effort must be made to raise your vibrations to the level of sun and moon worlds—that is, to the astral level. The signs of this happening are your physical body will start to vibrate or you will have a very warm feeling within your forehead area or you will hear a sound like a cork popping.

Now you must not get nervous or uncomfortable. If you can hold your nerve for a short period, the inner Master will appear to give darshan, or he may lead you to some spiritual journey. You may have noticed that some sci-fi films feature a spiritual man who has some powers; when he concentrates, a "spiritual ball of light" appears in front of him physically. This ball, with its magnificent lights, begins to circle. As long as his concentration is strong, the ball moves in a continuous circle.

But once he begins to lose his concentration, the ball also disappears. Do you know you are having the same experience when you are having this warm feeling within your forehead? Movie-makers make the experience more attractive by expressing it on the physical level. Miracles are another example of Spirit in action. Any person can create miracles, provided he or she is an open channel for Spirit. You walk in any direction, and miracles will follow.

Any word you utter, Spirit becomes obliged to execute your spoken dialogue because Spirit knows you are an expression of love and the Spirit of God. To you, this is normal, as you are living within Spirit all the time. But to others, these are miracles. You have gone beyond the amusement of mind. You do not ask for anything for yourself because nothing on the physical level attracts you. But you can ask for others, if you think they are worthy of receiving it.

Why should you ask for anything when everything is provided without you asking?! Your very near and dear relationship is with God. You are inseparable, being part of it. All else is illusion. When you become aware of this relationship with God, then how can you afford to hold any other relationship, which is painful and an illusion? Illusion means something temporary or unreal or created for your experience on the physical level. It often attracts the mind. World attachments come into play.

There is joy, but very soon, this joy turns in to pain. As the saying goes, no pain, no gain. Out of this pain and gain, we have spiritual experience. Once you understand this and find your way out, then you become the way shower. You can create miracles too. Spirit does not hide or deny anything from us. It is us who do not believe its existence. To those who believe, it appears with little effort because nothing is nearer to you than Spirit.

You are part of it. The human mind is always in search of the horizon far away and tries to reach it by physical means. Will it ever find what it is looking for? This is the question. You are always in the centre of it. When this realisation comes, all you can do is laugh at yourself. You know it is Spirit, and so are you. All these millennia, you have been running away from your own self. This is the riddle of you and God.

Spirit

I am. I am. I am the only way, being the essence of God. There is no other way or path that leads directly to the centre of God. Without me ("Spirit") you cannot move, and you would be in a state of suspension for millions of years. Spirit is always on the move. Everything moves and has its being in the worlds of God. I am infinite, without any limits or boundaries. I am present at every corner of all the universes. Every single soul represents my presence.

I am within each particle of soil; otherwise, nothing would grow. I breathe through the soil so all the vegetation can grow. I breathe through you, and you breathe through me, and the circle is complete. It is a continuous and everlasting circle. For your guidance, many times I appear to you through symbols. You must learn to establish the message within each symbol. I will give information about your future or a warning to be alert of something or some weakness on your part, which you need to work on.

The answers to your questions may be given in symbols. Many times, a direct answer is not suitable, as it could put you out of balance. This is my way of conveying the message. Those who are open channels to Spirit do not have any questions; nor are they seeking any answers, as they dwell in the spiritual fountain within. This is where the answer is given before the question arises. These are the people who are capable of answering the questions of others.

They are the expression of Spirit. The followers of any religions will never have direct experience of Spirit because they only express part of it. They do not believe I am still live. As long as I am live, everything exists. Otherwise, everything would turn to dust and non-existence. I am Spirit. All religious leaders are failing their followers by dictating to them to find me through material symbols or by saying, "We are the only way."

When they say, "We are the only way," they leave no breathing space for me ("God") in their followers. As soon as this is done, the direct link is closed. I am everywhere and within each soul, no more or less to any soul. The same applies to all religions. They are all part of me. But sadly, they only try to express a part of me. When they express me fully, they will become live as they were in the beginning. In the beginning, every religion is live. It is not the religion that is or was "live".

It is the spiritual saint who appeared in some part of the world to give the spiritual message. After the saint has gone, the followers create the religion on the basis of the given message and the sincerity of the regard they have for this person. Later it becomes less of Spirit and more political, to control the followers. Material symbols are used to express Spirit, instead of leading the followers to experience Spirit directly. Let's take some examples.

One religion does not consider any person a follower, unless his or her natural hairs are maintained and he or she wears certain symbols. That religion's message is good, but the maintenance of the spiritual message is totally lost. If some awakened person tries to lead, he or she is ignored or ridiculed to silence him or her. People feel more secure having their being in the past, when I always live in present. I moved from that spot where they are dwelling today long ago.

Another religion recommends that the followers must pray five times a day. How can you remember me only for five times a day, when I do not forget you for a single moment of the day or night? Otherwise, you will never wake up. I am alive and kicking, as they say, all around you, all the time. You only have to open up to me to feel my presence. *I am the way;* for you *the way is within,* as we are one.

Another religion is famous for going door to door saying, "We are the only way, and salvation is only through us" (or through their spiritual leader). That leader left this world many centuries ago and has probably become the spiritual leader of many other religions. These saints do not limit themselves, as they are infinite in the spiritual worlds. If this religion is the only way and it runs the show, then, as Spirit, who am I?

These people limit themselves and stop others from venturing into the spiritual worlds. By misguiding someone, you become liable for his or her wrongfully created karmas. In Asia, there are numerous religions using hundreds of symbols and rituals. They are so entangled in these practises that they have forgotten their true goal. Any religion practising these rituals and symbols is only representing a part of *me*.

The religion or its followers will never succeed in having a solid spiritual experience. Instead they become story-tellers. "I Am" as Spirit will be out of their reach because they don't want to know me. I am within and closer than your breath or heartbeat. You will know me the day you become one with me to say, "I am Spirit."

SPIRITUAL UNFOLDMENT

This is the journey of soul since it has left the soul plane and entered into the lower worlds. It entered as inexperienced and begins to "fold" itself with karma. It was given only very few karmas by the "Lord of Karma" so as to open its account in this world. As we are all aware, most of us begin our journey in the lower forms of lives. In these lower lives, we hardly create any or not many karmas.

For example, a plant—having its being in one place and not interfering physically or mentally with others—is unable to create many karmas, apart from gaining an experience. A tree will have the most experience, as it learns a lot of patience by being in one place for hundreds of years—unless its lifespan is cut short by humans. I have seen a few trees in the Golden Temple of Amritsar, India, and historically they are over 500 years of age. At present, they are still as healthy as ever they can be.

Being in one place, we can learn so many lessons. All the weather takes its toll, and the only protection they have is the umbrella of blue sky. That means no protection from anything. We all have been through this journey and succeeded, eventually taking the form of human shield. With all this "tree" patience experience, we still moan and groan. During our time as lower forms of life, we were passive. Now at present, we are very active mentally.

Due to this activeness, we have become aggressive and have adapted non-tolerance, and we lose our patience at every opportunity. What is unfoldment? First as an experience, we have folded into the lower worlds by creating lots of karma. Now with lots of experience, we want to unfold spiritually. At present, our spiritual knowledge is giving us the nudge that we are more than this physical body. We begin to meditate and ask ourselves question, what could be the way out?

We love to be in the presence of those people who are more spiritually awake. You can talk or listen to this spiritual interest for hours. This will lead us to become a spiritual Seeker, when before, we were seeking everything on material basis. You have lost your interest in the material things, but coming to this spiritual interest has not been so easy. With a spiritual search, you have managed to find a spiritual Master. You thought that, now, your life was going to be easy, but you experience the opposite.

What could be the reason for this? There is a task for the Master to help you unfold spiritually. He wants to make sure that you have learned every experience you require. Master helps you to unfold spiritually, very similarly to a flower as it opens its petals one by one. You are provided with five passions of the mind as a helping hand to gain this experience. Those who think of these five passions as enemies will never have any solid spiritual success.

In the beginning you thought that all these mind passions were under your control. When the spiritual Master tested you from different directions, it did not take long to learn that you were nowhere near the mark of any command over them. This is where the majority of us fail, thinking in the terms of control. Rather, the approach should be to balance them out and lead your life in balance. Once we have this balance in our lives, we will move in the direction of spiritual unfoldment.

We always talk of having the experience of bliss state, so what is this bliss state? It is the total balance of our five passions and the flow of Spirit within. In the bliss state, you are totally relaxed beyond your physical imagination. Once you've made a habit of living in this state of consciousness—also known as "being yourself" in a true sense of spirituality—nothing bothers you. All the problems we used to complain about in the past, now you probably laugh at them.

There is no such thing as problem in life. There are a few situations that are not in our favour; otherwise, problems are non-existent. These situations, what we call problems, are not bothering the person standing next to you, so we can draw some conclusions from that. I have given some explanation in "The Way to God" chapter called "Problems are Zero". We can compare the journey of soul with any seed of a plant. The physical seed is produced by any plant, while the soul is the creation of God.

In theory the journey of any soul is not much different from the journey of a seed. Seeds are produced by the billions each year, but how many manage to become plants? Only a small percentage. The majority of them are used as bird feed or turned into flour for cooking, while a good percentage rot away. This does not apply to any soul, as soul is here to stay and experience. But one thing is common. Not many souls manage to set themselves free spiritually, while the majority of them are struggling.

Still we take the example of a successful seed. The seed is planted or grown itself in the wild. The plant begins to appear out of the soil. A few leaves appear and then grow a little higher, and in the season of spring, it is ready to flower. Notice that the majority of plants are green in colour during their youth. Then, with experience, it's time to unfold and show this world what they can produce. Now it is totally unbelievable what nature can produce out of a little green plant—yellow, red, pink, and white flowers.

We admire this beauty and fragrance of nature. This is the unfoldment of this plant and its successful journey. We, as soul, have a rather long journey. Now, going back to the control over the five passions—those you once thought you had control over. When Master put you through different tests, you will realise nothing is in your control, as they will be running all over you. The Master will test you from a point you have never thought of. There are no shortcuts to this spiritual journey.

The Master will make sure that you have become the knower. The spiritual exercises given earlier are a great helping hand to materialise your spiritual goals. Furthermore, it was recommended to have a "silence fast"—that is, to stay silent most of the day. It will bring lots of stillness to your mind.

The next one will be to learn how to blank your mind. It is so easy. This can be practised while sitting still or standing or while walking. Now, the procedure is not to think.

As we are all aware, the mind is thinking all the time. But this time, you are conditioning your mind not to think. Do you know that you are thinking, even when you are not thinking? This is something we have to learn. Driving a car makes a good analogy. Although we are driving at a very high speed, at some point, we have to change the gear to the neutral position. So, if you can work on this, you will have lots of success. Here are some steps you can follow.

You are practising to be in the position of being God. Someone rings me the other day, saying that it is a good experience to act as a God for the day. I must clarify that it is not just for a day; you must practise every day and forever to have any serious spiritual success.

1. You already are practising the food or mental fast.
2. You are practising to remain silent for a day once every week.
3. Last, you are beginning to learn how to blank your mind. Now, I think you have enough spiritual tools to practise. Otherwise, I have an unlimited number of tools in my spiritual bag to give.

This is the path of enlightenment, as I mentioned very recently. I have a cassette of Paul Ji, where he mentions to the effect that this path is designed to train you as a saint. When it comes to this training, you'd better be prepared to become alone but never lonely, as the presence of Master is always with you. Your companion will be your spiritual Master and many spiritual beings. Now when you have such companions, who wants to deal with so many on the physical level?

You will be dwelling in a bliss state; at the same time, you will be physical too. The teachings have been the same as ever, but for last few years we practised to relax. While you people are practising to learn how to be in the position of God, at the same time, I have been practising, nowadays, how to relax like you do. God does not interfere within the journey of any soul; it lets the soul learn at its own pace. Soul itself is beyond time.

But when we are talking about the physical lifespan, then definitely, we have limited time. The present Master acts the same way as God. He will not interfere in anyone's life but to convey its message. When you have succeeded in being in the presence of God all the time, then no one will have to tell you that you have unfolded spiritually. You will know yourself, as you will have become the knower of truth.

The word we stress quite often is *unfoldment*. You will learn there was nothing to unfold or to achieve. You have just become aware that you have been part of God all the time. If you can catch this point—spirituality cannot be taught but it can be caught (it comes to you like a cat coming on silent feet to catch its prey)—you won't even have to practise anything.

You will have become the knower of this spiritual truth, and it is known as instant realisation. This is why Master always said, "I can give this realisation to any one at any time, provided the Seeker is ready to live this experience." Now, the question is, do you want to unfold spiritually the hard way or do you just want to walk into this everlasting experience?

The choice is yours.

ULTIMATE

What could be the ultimate goal or achievement for us? This is the question. As we enter into this world or just before, some parents are already working on their child's future. Most likely, plans are to make their child, what they wanted to be in life but, due to many circumstances, could not achieve. We are responsible for the well-being of our children. But that does not mean we have to impose our dictates on the child's future. I have seen many people on TV during drama or dancing competitions.

To send children to drama or dancing schools is very common. When a child is sent to drama classes, it means that parents, at one time, wanted to become movie stars; now they want to live their dream through their children. This is to satisfy the minds of parents. The child, being innocent and naïve, is willing to follow the dictates of parents. The child begins to feel the natural ability to fulfil this task, which has been designed or fabricated by the parents.

This means we have silenced the free will of the child. Every single child or soul comes into this world to fulfil some destiny big or small. We are responsible for bringing up and educating our children. However, as the child grows older in age and having had the education, the child adopts a way of life to which he or she feels naturally attracted or has the ability to follow. We never know what the child can do. We should not silence the child's individuality. Let the child develop his or her own personality.

What the child achieves or becomes could be less than your expectations or could go way beyond your expectations. What could be our goal in life? Do we want to become doctors, politicians, or engineers? Many of us cannot think beyond this, due to our circumstances. We may not think that there is something beyond these goals that can be achieved, while doing our physical chores. That is to achieve spiritual enlightenment.

I was lucky, or unlucky, as my parents were not very educated and were not concerned about achieving something in life. This was unlucky for me, as they could not guide me on the physical level. But on the other hand, I was lucky, as I had the opportunity to do whatever I wanted to do in life. So, I educated myself the way I wanted to and worked the way I wanted, and I've had a fair amount of success too. On the other hand, I had a dream within myself to know and experience God in this lifetime.

I developed my personality around that which is very silent and exciting at the same time. As I travelled through the inner worlds, I felt more like a balanced individual. We are happy if we do something worthwhile in life. Our goals are so small; we become satisfied with the smallest milestones. Some are able to buy a number of properties and are happy to be called landlords. It is the same with politicians and those whose careers are in other fields.

Some can manage to leave their name in this world to be remembered for centuries. However, when we come to the end of our life, we pause for a second and think, *Did I achieve anything that I can take with me to the worlds beyond?* We have not achieved anything that can be taken with us because we have been too busy or involved in physical responsibilities. We never thought of looking beyond or considering what it could be. Very rarely do people talk about "the far country" or worlds beyond.

Even if we do think about it, we feel it is beyond our reach, or we don't have the ability to see it. Most of us think that Jesus, Guru Nanak, Buddha, or Mohammad did it, and there is no way we can do something similar. Yes, they were special people and individuals in their own ways. Krishna of Hinduism is the oldest, and Buddha is second. Jesus Christ is third in line, and his followers claim he is the only one to give salvation to this world. According to this theory, Mohammad should not be here.

But he appeared as a new prophet, and now he has millions of followers. Guru Nanak appeared in the fifteenth century, and now he also has millions of followers. All these prophets appeared in this world time after time. There is no end to it. "God-sent men" will be coming until the end of this world. Who knows who will appear in which part of the world? Never limit yourself by saying, "I cannot do this." Every single person in this world is equal in the eyes of God, as it has given you the same abilities as anyone else.

God wants every single soul in this world and beyond to unfold spiritually in order to become assistants and to take responsibility. It surprises me that we are not told openly by our elders to follow in the footsteps of our creator. No one can become a second God, but it has sent us into the lower worlds to educate ourselves spiritually—so that we can participate in its endeavour in the higher worlds. It has given us the ability to do this, and like any parent, God wants us to be successful as its own children.

This should be our ultimate goal.

THE WRATH OF GOD

Every single person in this world, especially those who are religious, is afraid of these three words. All religions stress that their followers should fear the "wrath of God", and the followers tell the same to others. If you do something wrong, be prepared to reap what you sow. In a sense, this is the backbone of all religions; otherwise, they may not even exist. If there is no fear, who wants to know what religion is? Or what are the benefits of being a religious person?

If you know what God is—not as a religious person but in reality, which is very difficult to know—then probably you'll be surprised to learn that the expression of these three words is not true. All religious concepts expressing these three words are far from the truth. The expression shows very clearly that these religions or their founders have never been close to the reality or in the presence of God. This is why they always say or express that God is totally out of reach or knowing.

To the contrary, the same religion also says that God is within each individual as soul or Spirit. God has created soul in its own image to express its presence everywhere. Soul is the pure image of God, very similar to the way we see the image of our physical form in a mirror or water. If we can see our own physical form reflected in a mirror, then who is stopping you from seeing God in each soul? The answer is quite simple, because God has made it very simple and easy to approach.

We have become quite lazy. We can travel thousands of miles for our interests, but we're unable to cross a hair's breadth distance. It is a well-known fact that, if something is given free in life, it will never be appreciated as much as if it is earned. You are given something you are not interested in, even though your gift is very valuable. God has given part of itself to each individual to know or feel its presence. Now, how many are interested in doing that? Very few or none.

We have created a wall between its presence and ourselves because our interests are somewhere else. As I walk along in life, I come across some faces, and through their expressions, I can see God walking on the streets. I have a habit of looking at anyone once, whoever comes within my sight. I will only look twice if I see the spiritual spark in a person's eyes. Then I can see the presence of God walking among us in this world. This expression could be through a male, female, or child, or it could be in a dog or a cat.

At that time, these individuals may not know what they are expressing, and their thoughts may be miles away from knowing this. But at that present moment, they were the carriers of this spark within. Children do this all the time because they are so innocent and pure and don't know what negativity or fear is. Do you know? If a child is sitting next to a lion, tiger, or dog, this child may catch the tail of the cat or dog and laugh at the same time.

In return, I expect this animal not to react with anger because animals only react upon our vibrations of fear or grudge. I have seen this personally. We create our own fears. This is where the expression comes in action known as the "wrath of God". I must clear this point first. There is no such thing as wrath of God. As I said earlier, the majority of religions have not touched the face of God to know what actually God is. God has created souls in its own image to experience.

So as to become assistants in its cause in the higher planes, as well as in lower planes. These include saints or a Master of a given time, created to show the way to souls who are seeking the truth. Soul is in a neutral state of consciousness as God. God has created everything for the soul to experience. Then how can it destroy or have wrath for the soul? This is where the schooling comes in and all the ups or downs exist. God dwells in the pure spiritual worlds, which are beyond matter, energy, space or time.

These spiritual worlds are everlasting beyond any effect, but God also created the lower worlds, which are not permanent and are subject to changes. Soul is eternal, and it cannot be seen visually. So, God has provided the lower bodies as clothing, so it can be seen visually. Soul has four other bodies as a cover or to express and experience on each spiritual plane, also known as lower bodies. These bodies are subject to the lower planes and are also subject to suffering.

These bodies are responsible for creating the reasons for the wrath of God to take place. Wrath of God is our own creation and suffering. Now we will see how we create and face the wrath of God and then ask mercy for our own doings. God is not in the position to forgive. If God does forgive, then the whole system will be out of balance, and justice won't be done. As the saying goes, there is no smoke without fire, so this wrath does not come out of nowhere.

A single person cannot be responsible for big disasters. It is always a group of people who create negative karma on a massive scale without any due care. If you look at any place where large disasters took place and go into the background of the places or the people who lived there, you will find lots of wrong-doings. I always try to look behind the curtains to find the truth. I will give you a very recent example. This situation can be related as the wrath of God.

On 15 June 2013, big floods took place in Uttara-khand, India. It was a total wipe-out of the buildings, including all well-known temples, and people were trapped for days. Approximately 6,000 people lost their lives. First, this proves that God is not living in the buildings known as temples. Secondly, let's consider the people who we thought were poor and who we normally hired as helping hands to climb the mountains to visit these temples.

During this situation, I would expect them to help every person they could, as the visitors are their bread and butter. Instead, they robbed every single person who came in their way and emptied the pockets of the dead. They stole gold and sexually assaulted the females. This is how our mind works. It does not matter how bad the situation we are going through is; we always have careless attitudes and give no thought of any karma.

These people were in the middle of this experience known as "wrath of God", and despite this, they did not have any pity on the people experiencing the wrath alongside them. Now is the time to remind everyone why God does not show any mercy in these situations; it knows they will never learn. Now who is responsible for this creation or show of wrath? It is not God, as many or almost everyone believes.

God has created the lower worlds, and it also has appointed rulers or hierarchy of Masters for each plane to keep everything in balance. The Lord of Karma is appointed on the astral plane to look after the affairs of physical. Whenever the Lord of Karma notices that situations or places are out of balance, it shows who is in command. This is the wrath of total karma backfiring on us, and it is often misunderstood as the "wrath of God".

"We reap only, what we sow"

The maladjustment created by us, the commanding force take action to bring back balance; only then we say it is the wrath of God, when it was our own creation. People do fear when they have to face the wrath of God, but they are not afraid when they create the situations for it to happen. All the eruptions of volcanoes, tornados, or excessive water are the signs of this.

Many situations take place due to the global warming; again, we are responsible for that too. Nowadays there are so many incidents occurring throughout this world of a person carrying dangerous weapons and choosing various places to shoot a number of unknown and innocent people without care. Can you imagine the amount of karma that has been created by this one person?

And some people are doing this in the name of their religion. There is no thought given to the consequences. The same goes for those who take money or expensive gifts or property and do not wish to pay back their debt in time. They will face the penalty sooner or later. A very famous writer Sir Walter Scott wrote this famous line:

"Oh, what a tangled web, we weave."

Now if we look into the backgrounds of the people who create these massacres, no one is born to have this kind of unbalanced mind or to be in this position with a careless attitude. As a child, everyone is born innocent, an expression of God. But as children grow, with years, the mind gets stronger or weaker. Some people will take advantage of this innocence and drive you up the wall. Then you either get depressed or go berserk mentally to take revenge and go on a spree of killings to let go of your anger on anyone who comes your way.

Again, someone is responsible behind this person's mental pressure. No one cares about creating karma. And the majority of those who are responsible for guiding us—religious leaders or priests—are greedy and worse than normal people on the scale of karma. Little eruptions in this world or broken stars within a galaxy are normal and happen for reasons. Although temporary, God is not willing to destroy these lower worlds; minor unbalances are possible.

This universe is good enough to live for humans and vegetation for a long time yet. One day will come when this universe will not be fit for the humans or vegetation. For this, God will not be responsible. It will be the result of humans experimenting beyond nature and will destroy the goodness of this earth. It will become barren land, and oxygen will only exist just to hold the planet together. Those souls who have found their way back by following the Master of the time will be lucky.

Others will be put to sleep in physical terms or in a bliss state in spiritual terms. Then goodness of Spirit will be showered on "New Earth Planet" to begin once more Satya-Yuga or Golden-Age. Now you may be wondering, what mess humans could create that it would come to the point that God had to evacuate all the souls. That is correct, and it was all expected as well by its creator; after all, it was training ground for souls. It is similar to any football ground, when match is over, it is left empty and alone.

We know Kal is or will get stronger by day. But due to scientific experiments, all the sciences will merge into real religion, and people will become soul travellers. The majority of them will find their way back into the higher planes. The basic requirement will be that science has to break the time and speed barrier to zero zone for any basic travelling. Furthermore, there are a number of zero zones for each higher plane. All the present known or so-called dominating religions will fade away with time.

As they will have nothing to offer, apart from their hollow promises. Religious scriptures given by their respective prophets are correct, but nowadays, they are misinterpreted to satisfy their materialistic needs. The literature of science will almost sound like religion because of their spiritual findings. Nowadays, people are excited about mobile phones and the internet. In future people will have a hobby of travelling to and exploring higher planes.

The wisest person will be the one, who has travelled farther than anyone else. Almost everyone will be a soul traveller, and those who did not manage will be taken back to the continuation of isness state—until the lower worlds are ready as they were in the beginning of Satya-Yuga, and a new Golden-Age will begin.

LOVE FORCE

In the early days, Paul Ji taught us the art of love force, which I feel at present is lost to some extent. God itself is pure love. It is this love reaching from "IT" to us as flow, and it returns to it, also known as sound. It is God's love that sustains all the universes. It is this continuous and everlasting love that we are all part of. Love force, when applied on a neutral basis or for the "good of the whole", can work wonders, known as miracles.

This love is also known as Spirit, and we all are open channels for the Spirit. I don't think anyone can imagine the power of this love force because it is beyond knowing. We must be full of love, before its application to bring changes for the good of the whole. Otherwise, it will not work; if your vibrations are not pure, the results you want to see will not materialise. This pure love force supersedes the mental power. Mental force is also very powerful when applied with full concentration.

You must have seen some programmes on TV or some live shows. A trained person with mental faculties can focus on some metal object, such as a spoon; he can move or bend this object without touch, when normally we cannot bend it this easily. Many trained people can misuse this mental faculty as well. I remember once Paul Ji mentioned he used to visit one cafe, and the owner hired someone who was trained in this mental art.

The man's job was to divert the minds of those passing by so that they would come into the cafe as customers. This type of mental manipulation can be done, but it is a violation of the spiritual law known as psychic space. There is always someone with whom we cannot get along. He or she will make an attempt to harm us in many ways. But being on the spiritual side, we do not want to react to this person's standards of thinking. We can choose to not react. Instead, we can apply this love force; it can work wonders.

This art of love is a gift from God to all humanity, but nowadays I notice we have lost this art over the years. Or we are not using it whole-heartedly, and it does not bring the results to our expectations. You must be full of love before any application of it, as I've said in previous discourses. If you are God, then what are you? You're full of love. Now you are in the driving seat. Now even before you apply this love force, you already know the results. In your attempt, you will never fail.

If you want to have eye contact with God, you have to be like God. It is our own fears that keep us away from it, and the outcome of any attempt made on our part is very poor. All the religions in this world claim that God is within each individual, but all the religious scholars also say that we cannot see or converse with God. To me these two statements do not add up. And if this is their belief, then I don't think they know what "love force" is. Application of this love force is totally beyond their knowing.

This is why they believe in prayers, which are never answered. The person who applies this love force to all without any condition will have the ability of spiritual gaze. Spiritual gaze is the power of your love flowing through your eyes to the others, which can be used to raise someone's vibrations or to heal someone. Spiritual Masters are naturally gifted with this power. This is why sometimes they are also known as eagle-eyed adepts.

People will notice your presence, and without knowing, they will feel the pull towards you. Your presence will be very similar to a magnet, which has a natural pull. A new-born child has this ability naturally. Once you see the child, you feel this love force. It does not matter how tired or angry you are or how much of any other difficult emotion you are experiencing; a cute little smile can conquer all of this, and you will feel happy and fresh.

This child's little smile or love force will force you to pick the child up or tickle or kiss as a gesture of love. This is the power of love force naturally used. You must make a habit of this application of love. Give your love to all unconditionally. You will be surprised to learn the results. As I've said many times, I am not a writer, but I manage to write lots because I apply this love force on a neutral basis. What is love force? It is Spirit. And what is Spirit? It is light and sound. And what is light and sound?

It is God itself. Now if you are one with God, what results will you be expecting? I do not expect any results because, if I am one with God, then God does all for me, even beyond my expectations. When you do not expect any results and leave everything in the hands of Spirit, only then does all materialise. All this that I write down comes out of this "love force". I never sit down to write anything ever. When this love force / Spirit guides me to write, only then do I sit down.

And above all, I never choose the subject; it is given to me. First, Spirit lets me know what the subject will be as "title". Then it gives me the love force—what to say on the subject. As I hold the pen in my hand, my physical speed is so slow when it comes to writing or typing I hardly manage to write what has been said. Then Spirit gives me breathing space because, at the end of the day, it is the message of Spirit that I want to convey to the Seekers.

During the mid-seventies, all of us did learn how to make use of or apply this love force; probably the older members will tell us. We used to feel as if we weren't walking but floating above the ground. That was the love force in action. But over the years, we have lost this art of loving, and many kinds of sufferings begin to appear. Give your love to all unconditionally, and all will be yours. The people who are against you will be pulled towards you naturally. Spirit works wonders.

Nothing can stand in the way of Spirit, as Spirit is so close to you. We all know that Spirit is all around us; much like with radio waves, whoever tunes to the correct frequency will get the signal. It will be the strength of your unconditional love known as your positive or neutral vibrations; what you can catch will be totally beyond your expectations. If you want to get stuck spiritually as many are, that is your decision too.

Never underestimate your ability.

Probably the Spirit cannot appear directly to anyone, but it can materialise anything if doing so is the requirement. Take this discourse as another exercise to practise on. Normally, it will use any person who is an open channel to the Spirit. Don't you think it should be **you**, provided you let the Spirit use you? In the early days, lots of people use to make remarks and approached you by saying, "I think you are special." Now when was the last time someone said this to you?

You are still the same person but minus the live spiritual flow. Revive yourself again. Practise the presence of your spiritual Master. Practise your spiritual exercises on a regular basis. And practise the presence of being part of God. Then I cannot even imagine what can stand in your way—not any problem or any person or any situation. Overall, who is the Master of these problems or situations? It is God itself. Without its permission, nothing exists.

But it has given free will to all, so everyone can have his or her being at his or her own conditions. At the same time, we will all pay the consequences according to our own decisions. You give free will to all, as it does. Apply your love force, and then all these people, problems, and situations will move along with you, without affecting you. "Let it be." With this let it be, you can move mountains. With this love force, you are live, and so are the others.

If Spirit is live and you are live too, then how can someone stand in your way who is not spiritually live? We always under-estimate the strength of love force and use our physical action and impaired mental judgement and often fail. I am sure many of you are using spiritual faculties and that, ever since you started, your life situations have improved. There will be times when you know that you are floating above on automation like an aeroplane; there is no comparison to this spiritual freedom.

Did you ever realise that it does not matter how negative we are or how this world is producing negativity? It does not affect God at all. It is beyond matter, energy, space, and time. Now can you imagine, if you are beyond all this, then how can anything affect you? All these negative situations are affecting you at present because you are part of them. Once you rise above, only then you will know what we are talking about here. You must learn to do everything on a neutral basis unconditionally.

You are an open channel to the Spirit, so I am not going to spell it out for you. Is that what you are? You will know yourself. The word *impossible* should not exist in your dictionary. Where a light is lit in the house, most likely the thieves won't enter the property because they'll know someone is awake. It's the same with the five passions of the mind. The Kal force won't enter your psychic space. Kal knows that you are awake spiritually. Love force is only possible if you are spiritually awake. Otherwise it is a house of horror and "darkness", and love force do not exist.

May this love force be with you.

YOUR SUCCESS OR FAILURE

Now you have read most of this book, it's about time to analyse your success or failure. Make use of your strong points and work towards your weaknesses. Those who have not made any effort so far "should know by now" why Spirit doesn't listen to your cries. If you want to remain in this maze, it is entirely your decision to do so. Maybe some people want to learn the hard way. In England, there are drains carrying all the domestic or commercial filth that lead to a manhole, and this manhole is full of darkness and filth.

Spirit can only help those who wish to move on with their lives. If you are someone who's decided to remain in the darkness and cry, all I can say is that you are under-estimating your ability. The people I am talking about here, they know who they are, should take this message in positive manner and move on to have success in life. All these drains and manholes, better known as problems, are the story of every house.

At one point, Guru Nanak said, "Nanak Dukhian sab Sansar" (Everyone in this world is suffering or is in sorrow). Those who manage to face the facts with a smile are better off. Otherwise, an ocean of tears is waiting for you. All these problems or situations are part of darkness or Kal. The word *Kal* means "black" or "dark" or "negative". This word is used throughout this world to express the same. Many times, we are naive enough to walk into problems or create some, not knowing the consequences.

Or some are created for pleasure, but when they grow out of proportion, we begin to suffer, not knowing where turn to. We always expect someone else to take care of our problems, so we can feel free. Or we love to leave all our problems in the hands of Spirit. Now the question is, did Spirit or someone you relying on create these problems for you? The answer is they did not. So, when are you going to learn to face the facts?

This is exactly what Spirit wants to see in each of us—to feel and realise the responsibility that goes with all our actions. What can be the reaction of our actions to the others will be karma in our account. Being assistant means we know our responsibilities consciously. Once my manager told me at work, "If you make a mistake on a minor scale, then probably you will keep repeating it many times.

But if you go through the mistake fully, then probably you will remember it for rest of your life, and it will not be repeated many times over." As for the people who are not making any effort at present, I still see positivity in this message. That one day they will be the believers I can count on. I'll be proud to say, "Yes I know them." Now you may be wondering what your next task will be. Yes, in this case, you can write down your recent experiences or your recent learning.

"What are your success or failure points, since you have been following this path? I am sure that some of you are capable of writing a book. Pause for a while and go over your weaknesses and see how you can improve them. Your success points will be your strength to achieve your goal, and you can make the most of your weaknesses. And both your strong points and weaknesses will contribute overall.

SILENCE

Silence is golden. These words are often used. They mean nothing if you do not practise.

God itself lives in *silence*. That is why. It is beyond matter, energy, space, and time. This is why some people cannot hear it and many don't believe its existence.

When you are in *silence*, all time, space, and matter dissolve themselves, and you are in the presence of it.

Silence is the second name for inner communication.

Silence means you are totally lean within Spirit. You can meditate under the blue sky or in a jungle, no weather, animal, hunger, sickness will touch you.

Silence means all your external senses are closed, and you are directly within its presence. Then what is there that you cannot know? As long as you are living in the world of *chaos*, I don't think you will go very far, apart from a few glimpses or little experiences.

You must come to the condition of your sitting that all of your passions, thinking, and body are in *silence*. As long as something is ticking, very similar to your nerve, you will never have success.

You must practise to remain in *silence* and build a cloud of fog around you, so no one will ever know that you are here.

The whole creation came out of this *silence*.

Silence is golden. Many invitations to Kal disappear. That is why, I recommend this to those, who are above average in communicating. Try to have a *silence fast* once a week.

All I have written so far came out of *silence*.

As for all those who are not successful spiritually, it shows very clearly that they have not become part of this *silence* yet.

Sitting in *silence* is very peaceful. I sit in *silence*. Do you?

Happiness is in *silence*.

All sounds are created out of this *silence*.

All inventions came out of this *silence*.

All trees are standing in *silence* and having their being. We sit in their shadow because they are silent; if they were not, probably they would ask us to leave them alone.

The most powerful beings created by God, known as the *super souls*, are always in *silence*. They control all the universes with this *silence*.

The "Haiome" sound is part of this great *silence*.

I am the carrier of this *silence*. That is why I managed to remain silent for all these years.

Silence speaks louder than words.

This great *silence* does not cry, despite what happens in this world. Those who cry over every little tiddly will never know what this great *silence* is. Realisation comes later. Basic foundation is very important.

The day *silence* cries the whole world will be wiped away. The things or relations you most value will never be heard of. What are you going to do then? The answer is 'Nothing'. You have wasted your valuable time for nothing.

To know this *silence*, you have to be part of it first.

Silence is always live; all the noises come and die down with time.

At the end of this Kali-Yuga, this planet will remain in *silence* till its next allotted time.

The secret of living longevity is to remain in *silence* as much as possible.

The saints often train their very sincere and serious students as a discipline to remain in the dark room alone with little food. To have any serious success, practise this *silence* all day and night for forty days. We do nothing but expect the whole world to be in our pocket.

Cats hunt on *silent* feet, but you have to be silent to be hunted by the Spirit.

When I asked everyone to write something on the subject "what are you following?" the same question came into the minds of many: What do I write? That means you are not *silent* yet.

You can hear the birds singing early in the morning, when the majority of this world is sleeping. As soon as this world wakes up and there is chaos everywhere, these natural sounds are *silenced* by our noises.

Most saints try to remain sitting in one place, so their *silence* continues without fail. We do not manage to sit in one place because our minds are unstable. We feel irritated and get up. This is why every person cannot be a saint.

Eternal sound can only be heard when all is *silent*, not when you try to hear.

All priests will not hear this *silence* until or unless they switch to the next spiritual dimension.

The sea is calm and silent, but our polluted ideas break its *silence*.

All those who are *silent* "give". God gives to all. The sun gives light during the day, and the moon gives its light at night, but those who receive are always complaining. This means they are never satisfied.

You can hear the silent flute on the soul plane because there is everlasting *silence*.

Spiritual Master is always watching *silently* by standing next to you.

All the religions have one thing in common. They believe that their spiritual Master or Masters are alive, although some have passed away a few thousand years ago. No believer has the power to put a stop to the reincarnation of these great beings. They have done their duty and are long gone, whilst their followers are still looking for them in churches, temples, and mosques. What resides within these places is hollow *silence*.

Followers who make requests with sincerity have their answers materialised through this great *silence*, providing they manage to raise their vibrations.

We kill animals without their consent to create food, and we draw milk out of their bodies, which is meant to be for their siblings. They are all *silent*. Humans, better known as the highest state of consciousness of God's creation, cry with every little pinch. We have not learnt how to give. We only know how to steal or grab.

I am the only pure channel of God. That is why I am *silent*. All pseudo-masters are trying to sell in the market what they don't have.

Humans cry at birth in this world because they are a part of this big chaos. They only go in *silence* when it's their last breath in this world. Those who manage to stay in *silence* are saints.

Wild animals don't have a permanent roof over their heads, and the birds are roaming free under the blue sky, yet they are *silent*.

Don't make the mistake of believing that all those who are very *silent* are saints. Some crooks, thieves, and back-stabbers are hiding behind this silence.

It may seem to be the end of this world for some due to many problems. When you walk through this experience with pain, our shadows are always *silent*.

The path of enlightenment is the result of this *silence*.

Silence speaks when words cannot.

You only speak when you know your words are better than your *silence*.

Silence can lead you to the inner level, when words can drag you down the hill.

If you do not understand the *silence* I am talking about, you will never understand my writing.

Always find time for *silence* out of your busy world.

The day you have turned your back on *silence*, you will be lost in a gigantic maze.

You must find inner happiness when in *silence*. If you are sad, then there is something wrong.

Silence is a spiritual virtue of success only a few fortunate ones can master.

Don't waste your words on people who don't want to know. Your powerful speech will be taken as nothing, when your *silence* may be more powerful.

You will only feel or know the nudge of Spirit when you are *silent*.

Silence is always better than meaningless dialogues.

Spiritual communication will only whisper in your ears when you are totally *silent*.

Silence—deaf people may find some frustration due to this disability, but they will never know how lucky they are not to hear lots of garbage.

Walk on the path to find *silence* within. You will never fail. Have you found your silence yet?

Silence is the key to inspirational creativity, which turns a simple thing into something extraordinary.

We have been told by our spiritual Masters that 90% of the spiritual teachings are at the inner level, and the remaining 10% are on the outer level. I just want to let you know that all the spiritual scriptures of this world written so far are not even 1% of this great *silence*.

You can experience the whole of eternity in a moment of *silence*.

Once you experience this *silence*, it will never let you down.

Be aware of the *silent* ones; they could be standing next to you.

With a smile you can solve many problems, and with *silence* you can avoid lots of problems.

Silence always tries to teach us something we are not aware of.

Let the *silence* take over your life. You will be born new spiritually.

Let the *silence* be a part of you. You will never be alone.

Telepathy is the second name to this *silence*. You can hear the whole world if you wish.

Those who are not *silent*, make other people's business as their own.

Those who are quick to answer in any conversation will never know what *silence* is.

The first stage is to know *silence*; the second stage is to walk and live in this silence.

The second name for a spiritual state of consciousness is *silence*.

Silence is the pure language of God; all else is part of illusion.

Silence can save you from lots of disappointing dialogues.

Within this *silence*, you can project yourself or walk into beingness state.

If we *silence* someone by force, that is sin.

With your *silence*, people may get the message more quickly than they would with words.

Do you reside in the world of *silence* or the world of chaos?

The destinies of those who are on the road of *silence* are not very far.

Silence is the key to tolerance and kindness.

The greatest men are often simple and *silent*, but they have extraordinary visions.

Silence does not mean yes to some or all questions. Sometimes it is better to let people find their own answers; otherwise, they will never know the truth.

When an opponent does a spell on you, do not react to accept; put the *silence* on your guard.

I was sitting and meditating; within this *silence* "came the light".

During sadness, people often experience *silence*. You can turn this into your strength.

Let us have a moment of *silence* for those who are struggling to be part of it.

Silence is balance.

Silence is patience.

Silence is your success.

Silence is the word of God.

In *silence*, you are with God, never a shadow.

In *silence*, you will see the spark of God in the eyes of child.

In *silence*, you are never alone.

In *silence*, you are never blind.

In *silence*, you don't think; you just be.

When I joined the teachings, I was almost *silent* for two years to understand the spiritual principles written by Paul Ji. Do not rush over the teachings. Have patience. Try to understand the principles and contemplate them in order to know them till you become the spiritual principle yourself.

We always rush in reading the monthly communication letter and then put that piece of paper to one side. It's the same with life. We are always in a rush; this rush leads you from one thing to another without any positive result. One day during this rush, you will come to know that your time is up. We always try to bite more than we can chew.

In silence ... every day is Christmas and a happy New Year.

Silence

Silence .... Silence

Silence ...... Silence ...... Silence

Silence ...... Silence ...... Silence ...... Silence ...... Silence

Silence ... Silence ... Silence ... Silence ...... Silence ...... Silence ...... Silence

Silence ... Silence ... Silence ... Silence ... Silence ... **until you are totally lost within this Silence** ....

I AM ALWAYS WITH YOU

I am "live", as always has been. I breathe through each of you. I breathe through air. I breathe through each particle of soil. Those who put some effort into knowing me, and through my present live channel, will see the live experience of my presence. I live in your dreams and close as to your heartbeat. There is no limit. I am everywhere. Once your spiritual vibrations are raised, my presence will shine through. What you see or hear in your visions is known as miracles to the normal human mind.

My presence is available in all the universes to all who believe in me. The sections in the remainder of this chapter describe experiences of a few of those who have made some effort recently, expressed in their own words to share with us what they have seen or heard. I am sure these experiences will inspire those who have been less fortunate in terms of what they have experienced so far. If you manage to put some more effort in the future, there is nothing that you cannot experience. I am live, so are you. Let us be one here and now as these people have been.

Consent: All these experiences have been printed with the consent of the recipients.

My Vision

One day I telephoned Sher-Ji to request a meeting. Sher-Ji asked to meet me in ten minutes, and I hurried over to his house. Sher-Ji met me with a big warm smile and said, "I would not worry if I could not see anything." I was surprised that he knew what I had been thinking and that I was going to ask him about my eyesight problem. He had been with me all the time. Later, I read in Sher-Ji's book that he and Darwin had worked so closely together. I had the same experience with Dar-Ji and Sher-Ji—that they were so close it was difficult for me to separate one from the other during my experience.

---- Rani, Greater London ---

Darshan of the Master

I had been experiencing stomach upsets for ten weeks. I visited my family doctor on 1 October 2013. He prescribed me some medication and wrote an urgent referral to the hospital. After two weeks wait, I was seen in the hospital. I had a general check-up, but hospital organised another test. That was two weeks later. The preparation was unpleasant, and the procedure was uncomfortable at times, despite the sedation.

The discomfort increased my anxiety a lot, and I was getting more and more worried. As I lay sideways, I had a pleasant feeling. I looked up and saw Sher-Ji coming towards me in a brilliant blue light. In his presence, I immediately lost all of my fear and all of my pain. I felt so happy and relieved. I recovered quickly from the test, and everything was normal. I am grateful that Sher-Ji came to see me when I needed him the most.

--- Mrs Seso Paul, Middlesex ---

Healings

With the blessings of Spirit, all the happenings in my life fall into the right place like a jigsaw puzzle. About one month ago, I went to the hospital for my early check-up, and after three to four days, I received letter from the hospital. I was to come in for another check-up on the other side of my body—they "saw something". I thought everything was fine, as I had been through this process and received successful treatment. Being human, I was bit worried and said to myself, "Not again." Then I requested that the Spirit give me the strength.

After my request I begin to feel comfortable. The day I went for my ultrasound in hospital, another friend went along with me for moral support. When I went inside for the ultrasound, I felt Sher-Ji's presence, and the doctor told me everything was clear. I am aware that Spirit is with me all the time, and it's a very wonderful feeling. I have no words to say thank you for your help with all your love and blessings.

--- Rita Gill Hounslow ---

Sher-Ji came to see me in person

During meditation, I imagined Sher-Ji wearing a white shirt. Some weeks afterwards, I decided to imagine Sher-Ji wearing a blue shirt. Five days after, I started to imagine Sher-Ji in a blue shirt. He came to visit me in person, and he was wearing the same blue shirt. I felt so happy that he was wearing a blue shirt as I had imagined.

--- Seeker ---

I saw the Master and light

I was heading home after attending our spiritual chant. As I was not feeling well, I asked for a lift to the nearest bus stop. I made a request for Sher-Ji to come with me. As I got off the bus and started walking home, I continued to sing spiritual verse. I felt a warm blue light surround me, and Sher-Ji appeared smiling. He said, "Okay." That light stayed with me till I reached home from the bus stop, which is about half a kilometre away. Thank you, Sher Ji, for your company.

--- Mrs Seso Paul ---

Spiritual eye

Dear Sher-Ji: I have been following the teachings for over thirty years and had the privilege to most of the spiritual experiences I can think of, such as dreams, light and sound, out of the body number of times with the help of spiritual Master. I believe, when you say everything is possible if we keep striving at it. I was following your instructions as guided in a very relaxed manner.

I was very fortunate today during my soul travel effort. Soul did not travel, but yourself in "radiant form" appeared on my third eye. Your image was within a sparkling silver-white colour. You gave me very wonderful smile, which is a memory to cherish, and I can visualise your smile as or when I wish. Thank you for your guidance and protection.

Your devoted Seeker in Spirit

--- Mr J. L. Middlesex, London ---

New Master

Dear Sher-Ji: Since Darwin Ji passed away, many circumstances have changed. I always had feelings only blessed ones will know the next Master. In one of my dreams, I saw you arranged a meeting. There were about sixty people, and you were giving a talk about forthcoming events, which I don't remember. In that dream, you and your wife were sitting together. And when the meeting finished, you and your wife started to levitate about five to six feet above ground. I believe it was a symbol that a new chapter has begun. Thank you.

--- Paramjit Gill, Hounslow, Middx ---

New Master

During the daytime, I was asking Darwin to let me know who is the new Master. During this experience, I was in the seminar as we were walking. Sher-Ji was leading us, and we were following him. Then Sher-Ji was on stage making a speech, and suddenly I woke up. This was good enough for me to know the truth. Thank you, Darwin Ji.

--- Mrs Narinder Tember, Hounslow, Middx ---

Good reading to you.

Sher Gill

Printed in the United States
By Bookmasters

Printed in the United States
By Bookmasters